A
Hemingway
Odyssey

A Hemingway Odyssey

SPECIAL PLACES IN HIS LIFE

H. LEA LAWRENCE

CUMBERLAND HOUSE
NASHVILLE, TENNESSEE

Copyright © 1992, 1999 by H. Lea Lawrence

Published by Cumberland House Publishing, Inc., 431 Harding Industrial Drive, Nashville, Tennessee 37211.

All photographs were taken by the author with the following exceptions. The photographs on pages 79, 80, 81, 95, 106, 107, 191, 192, and 195 were taken by Ardi Lawrence. The photograph on page 146 was taken by Joe Green.

Pages 7–10 constitute an extension of this copyright page.

Cover design by Gore Studio, Nashville, Tennessee.

Library of Congress Cataloging-in-Publication Data

Lawrence, H. Lea, 1930–
    [Prowling Papa's waters]
    A Hemingway Odyssey : special places in his life / H. Lea Lawrence.
        p.   cm.
    Originally published: Prowling Papa's waters. Atlanta : Longstreet, 1992.
    "Includes Hemingway's 1924 short story, Big two-hearted river."
    Includes bibliographical references and index.
    ISBN 1-58182-024-0 (pbk. : alk. paper)
    1. Hemingway, Ernest, 1899–1961—Homes and haunts. 2. Hemingway, Ernest, 1899–1961—Friends and associates. 3. Authors, American—20th century—Biography. 4. Fishing. I. Hemingway, Ernest, 1899–1961. Big two-hearted river. II. Title.
PS3515.E37Z68915   1999
813'.52—dc21
[B]   99-24090
                                                                              CIP

Printed in the United States of America

1 2 3 4 5 6 7 8—03 02 01 00 99

CONTENTS

ACKNOWLEDGMENTS

I WISH TO EXPRESS my thanks and appreciation to the individuals who provided me with information, assistance, and encouragement during the time I was doing research on this book: Shannon Besoyan, Capt. Roy Bosche, Violet and Amilio Bourghey, Carol Brandenberger, Marianne Busch, Elsa Spear Byron, Lino Castro, Peter Celliers, Howard A. Engle, Mike Evans, Angelika Fend, Herve Fournier, Amo Fricke, David Garcia Mendia, Andrea Ghiretti, Ralph Glidden, Tom and Carma Gronbeck, Doris Hemingway, Jack Hemingway, George Jaquet, Wendy Jaquet, Arnold Kessler, Bill Kovach, John Langley, Erica Leiben, Renato Manaigo, Gerhard Markus, Francois Michel, Gianni Milani, John Morris, Paul Nels, Silverio Nordone, David Richey, Sylvia Robards, Jan Roddy, Max Salzgeber, Maxwell Schneider, Susan Scott, Capt. Jerry Shunk, Jakober Sition, Georgia Smith, Karl Smith, Pedro Tellechea, Victor Urdiroz, Tina Walley, Elayne Wallis, Jessie Wasmuth, and to the staff of the Hemingway Room at the JFK Library: Megen Desnoyers, Lisa Middents, and Joe Dever.

Special thanks to Aubrey Watson for his custom photo work.

Grateful thanks is also due the following for permission to quote from several of Hemingway's writings:

Scattered excerpts from Hemingway's letters reprinted with permission of Scribner, a division of Simon & Schuster, Inc.,

permission of Charles Scribner's Sons, an imprint of Macmillan Publishing Company. Copyright © 1985 by Mary Hemingway, John Hemingway, Patrick Hemingway, and Gregory Hemingway.

Excerpts from MISADVENTURES OF A FLY FISHERMAN by Jack Hemingway reprinted with permission of Taylor Publishing Company. Copyright © 1986 by Jack Hemingway.

Excerpt from HIGH ON THE WILD by Lloyd R. Arnold (published by Grossett and Dunlap) reprinted with permission of Tillie Arnold. Copyright © by Tillie Arnold.

Excerpt from MY BROTHER, ERNEST HEMINGWAY by Leicester Hemingway (published by World Publishing Company) reprinted with permission of Doris Hemingway. Copyright © by Doris Hemingway.

Lines from holograph manuscript of Ernest Hemingway's GREEN HILLS OF AFRICA (originally cited in Carlos Baker's ERNEST HEMINGWAY: A LIFE STORY, Charles Scribner's Sons, 1969) reprinted with permission of the Hemingway estate. Copyright © by Mary Hemingway, John Hemingway, Patrick Hemingway, and Gregory Hemingway.

"The Day" (poem) by Ernest Hemingway, previously published in Peter Griffin's ALONG WITH YOUTH (Oxford Univ. Press, 1985) reprinted with permission of the Hemingway estate. Copyright © 1985 by Mary Hemingway, John Hemingway, Patrick Hemingway, and Gregory Hemingway.

Letter to James Gamble (April 27, 1919), previously published in Peter Griffin's ALONG WITH YOUTH (Oxford Univ. Press, 1985) reprinted with permission of the Hemingway estate. Copyright © 1985 by Mary Hemingway, John Hemingway, Patrick Hemingway, and Gregory Hemingway.

Excerpts from Ernest Hemingway's Notebook, 1916, previously published in Donald S. Johnson's "A Hike to Walloon Lake, June 10–21, 1916: A Diary," in *The American Fly Fisherman*, Summer 1989, reprinted with permission of the Hemingway estate. Copyright © by Mary Hemingway, John Hemingway, Patrick Hemingway, and Gregory Hemingway.

Excerpts from Ernest Hemingway's description of the *Pilar*, originally published in *Holiday* (1949), reprinted with permission of the Hemingway estate. Copyright © by Mary Hemingway, John Hemingway, Patrick Hemingway, and Gregory Hemingway.

"Big Two-Hearted River," Parts 1 and 2, reprinted with permission of Scribner, a Division of Simon & Schuster, Inc., from IN OUR TIME by Ernest Hemingway. Copyright © 1925 Charles Scribner's Sons. Copyright renewed 1953 by Ernest Hemingway.

INTRODUCTION

No ONE KNOWS WHAT thoughts were going through Ernest Hemingway's mind on the July morning in 1961 when he ended his life. However, ironic as it may seem, they may have been more about living than dying.

The act itself was possibly premeditated. Over the years he had often talked about suicide. If it was deliberate, the sequence from the moment he awoke until the last second may have been virtually mechanical. Quite obviously, the motive would have been preservation of his dignity, the quality in life he considered to be the most important of all. With body and mind failing, it is logical to assume that he wanted to close the final chapter before this too was taken away.

He did not fear death. As a child, he claimed to be "'fraid of nothing," and he displayed this characteristic throughout his life. It was also an attribute he gave to many of the characters in his books and short stories. An example from one of his best-known works comes to mind.

In *For Whom the Bell Tolls*, El Sordo, the rebel leader, is wounded and trapped on a hillside from which there is no escape. He looks up at the bright, high, blue early summer sky and knows it is the last time he will see it. But he is not afraid:

Dying was nothing and he had no picture of it nor fear of it in his mind. But living was a field of grain blowing in the wind on

11

the side of a hill. Living was a hawk in the sky. Living was an earthen jar of water in the dust of the threshing with the grain flailed out and the chaff blowing. Living was a horse between your legs and a carbine under one leg and a hill and a valley and a stream with trees along it and the far side of the valley and the hills beyond.

That was Hemingway's philosophy via El Sordo, but as anyone familiar with his life and works knows, living was also dropping a kicking grasshopper into the clear, cold water of the Fox River and feeling the sudden tug on the line as a trout took it; standing hip-deep in the swirling waters of the Clarks Fork of the Yellowstone with the jagged peaks of Pilot and Index as a backdrop; hiking through the beech forests of the Pyrenees to the headwaters of the Irati River; or watching a marlin make its slow majestic rise from the electric blue waters of the Gulf Stream.

Of the many sporting activities he enjoyed, none was more satisfying or enduring than fishing. As a child, after having been dressed and treated as a daughter by his mother since birth, fishing provided Hemingway with the first opportunity to display his maleness. By conducting one-on-one contests with trout, he was able to get away from those things that bothered him. The angling adventures of his youth also served as an inspiration for some of his early stories and forged an enduring bond between fishing and his writing. Later in life, fishing became even more important when it served as a release from the pressures and challenges of his profession. He said that the time spent on the water served to recharge his mental batteries and start the "juices" flowing again.

Living and fishing and happy times in Hemingway's life are what this book is about. Yet it is more than just a chronicle of his adventures and experiences and what he had to say about them. Included also are my observations and impressions gathered in the rather lengthy odyssey that took me to the special places in his life. It is a meld of the two views that provides an overview of the then and now.

A century has passed since Hemingway came into the world, and nearly forty years since he departed it. Many things changed during his lifetime, and many have occurred since. Surprisingly, though, I discovered in my travels a few places where time seems to have stood still. Relatively so, at least.

It is likely that the idea of writing about Hemingway was implanted in my mind long before I became aware of it. I read "Big Two-Hearted River" as a teenager and related to it strongly. Some years later, after my world had expanded and I'd finished a hitch in the service, I read the short story again and found that I had even greater affinity with it. Like Hemingway, I grew up fishing for trout, except instead of Michigan, the southern Appalachians of North Carolina and Tennessee were my territory. When I was discharged from the army, one of the first things I did was spend several days camping on one of my favorite streams. I savored the freedom and the solitude, and the image of Nick Adams returned sharp and clear. The difference was that I had not been traumatized by war, unless serving as a guinea pig in a series of atomic bomb tests in the Nevada desert somehow qualifies. At any rate, no personal demons interrupted my homecoming outing.

A dozen or so years later, when I saw the Gulf Stream for the first time, the idea was pushed closer to the front of my mind. By then I'd read almost everything Hemingway had written, including an *Esquire* magazine article titled "On the Blue Water," which contained the nucleus for his Pulitzer Prize–winning *The Old Man and the Sea*. During the long run out from Oregon Inlet on North Carolina's Outer Banks, I recalled it and felt I could anticipate the "great river." I couldn't. When the iridescent, azure flow finally came into view, I was overwhelmed by its majesty. On the many occasions I've seen it since, the thrill has never diminished.

My original idea was to write an article about fishing around Bimini in the Bahamas and describe some of Hemingway's adventures in the surrounding waters. For reasons I don't remember, that plan failed to work out, but I continued to want to write about the great writer. The more I thought about it, the greater that desire became. I considered adding the Keys and Cuba to the story, but soon other locations—Michigan, Wyoming, and Idaho—started crowding for attention. Next were Spain, Switzerland, Austria, and Italy. There was no stopping this idea. It was a juggernaut that quickly moved far beyond the usual length considered appropriate for an article. Suddenly, instead of dealing with one segment of his career, I had all of it in tow.

Hemingway spent a lot of time fishing in many places, and from boyhood until his last years he constantly sought out new places to explore. Following his footsteps precisely is an impossible task, of course, because some of his angling haunts are not readily accessible. Cuba is one. (Fortunately, I was there before the travel ban was imposed by the U.S. government.) Kenya, which is covered lightly here, is another. Since I am familiar with other prime fishing areas in the nearby Indian Ocean, however, regions that offer opportunities similar to those found off Mombasa, I could easily relate to the African experience.

This project has been enjoyable in all respects and no doubt enviable. I came away from Hemingway's special places with a wealth of memories. It was also satisfying to find that a few are still remote, such as some mountain streams where one can still find privacy. Others, such as those in the Bahamas, offer a similar benefit, except here privacy is assured by the vastness of the open sea.

Hemingway insisted that a good story had to include three elements: the time, the place, and how the weather was. I hope the following pages will supply all of these.

PART 1

Michigan

1

TALE OF
THE FOX

EARLY OCTOBER ON THE Fox River, watching fluffy snowflakes
drift down slowly onto the water's surface. It's like a mayfly hatch
in reverse, and I wonder what the trout think of it.

An hour ago it was calm and bright. Full sunlight illuminated
the gypsy colors in the trees, and the scent in the air was vintage
autumn. Then a cold wind picked up, and within minutes a
leaden curtain pulled across the sky. Weather on the Upper
Peninsula of Michigan is seldom predictable, so this preview of
winter is no surprise. My bet is that tomorrow it will again be
warm and beautiful.

The Fox is typical of most Michigan streams, fairly narrow,
channeled and swift, and not at all like the brook trout streams
of my youth. Those were very small creeks that tumbled down
out of the mountains and often could be almost stepped across.
The biggest brookie I ever caught from one was barely ten inches
long, which classified as a lunker. The average size was only six
to seven inches. But they were numerous and eager to bite, and
for a kid, that was the most important thing.

The spot I'm in fits the description of the one at which Nick Adams pitched his tent in "Big Two-Hearted River." I'm sure many others in the vicinity also would, since that part of the story and the name of the river are fictionalized. Hemingway used the Fox as the location but preferred the name of another Upper Peninsula stream, the Two-Hearted River, for the title. It sounded more like poetry, he said.

Other parts of the story are more factual, such as Nick's arrival by train in Seney and his walk of a dozen or so miles on an old logging track before detouring through the woods to the river. The present road probably follows about the same route. Nick camped about a quarter-mile off the road near where the Big Fox and Little Fox forks meet.

Nick's adventure took place more than seventy years ago when most parts of the Upper Peninsula were seldom visited by outsiders. The fishing was excellent in almost all of the streams and rivers. At that time the Fox contained both rainbow and brook trout. Today, it's managed primarily for brookies. Fishing is still good in the river, but nothing like it was in 1919. That was the year Hemingway was joined by two of his friends, Jock Pentecost and Al Walker, for the fishing trip that served as the inspiration for the famous story. Afterward, he described it in a letter to Howell Jenkins, another fishing pal:

Jock and Al Walker and I just got back from Seney. The Fox is priceless. The big fox is about 4 or five times as large as the Black and has ponds 40 feet across. The little Fox is about the size of the Black and lousy with them. Jock caught one that weighed 2 lbs 15 and a half of the inches. I got one 15 inches on the fly! Also one 14 inches. We caught about 200 and were gone a week. We were only 15 miles from the Pictured Rocks on Lake Superior. Gad that is great country. . . . I lost one on the Little Fox below an old dam that was the biggest trout I've ever seen. I was up in some old timbers and it was a case of horse out. I got about half of him out of wasser and my hook broke at the shank!

It's still great country, but the best fishing is no longer on the upper portion of the Fox. Perhaps it never was, but there's no way to tell. A section of the river a few miles below the bridge on Highway 28 at Seney may always have held that distinction. This is where the river enters a low, marshy area and scatters into many fingers or channels that on a map might resemble the frayed end of a rope. It's called The Spreads, and foot travel is virtually impossible. The only feasible way to fish it is by canoe. This restricted access has kept it isolated and helped preserve what is said to be the best native brook trout fishing in the state. Catches of twelve to fourteen inches aren't uncommon and occasionally eighteen- to twenty-inch specimens show up.

I learned about it from Tom Gronbeck. Tom and his wife, Carma, own Northland Outfitters in Germfask, a few miles below where the Fox flows into the Manistique River. They have rental canoes and camping equipment and specialize in arranging float trips.

They offer a variety of options on several area rivers, but one of the best is a float that begins on the upper part of the Fox and ends at Germfask. This trip provides four to five days of fishing and camping in spectacular country—not to mention a chance to spend plenty of time in The Spreads.

◆　　◆　　◆

"BIG TWO-HEARTED RIVER" MAY be the most analyzed—or over-analyzed—short story of our time. Scholars and critics find it to be full of symbolism, but generations of readers have been satisfied with seeing it simply as a touching, well-crafted story about a soldier returned from the war seeking peace and solitude on a trout stream. To me, the great appeal is that it's a human experience to which almost anyone can relate.

The story proved to be an early indicator of how fishing would influence Hemingway's works throughout his entire life. In a sense, fishing stories were the *alpha* and *omega* of his career. "Big Two-Hearted River," written in 1924 while he was in Europe, was the first of his writings to become well known. It marked his debut into American literature. The novel *The Old Man and the Sea,* written in Cuba in 1951, won him the Nobel Prize. It was the last major work of his lifetime.

In between those events, his fishing experiences provided a continuing source of material for his newspaper features and dispatches, magazine articles, short stories, and books. In addition, he carried on a lifelong stream of correspondence to friends and acquaintances on the subject.

Among the first letters were several sent to his father in August 1914, while he was with his mother on a vacation trip to Nantucket Island. In one of them he spoke of sailing on the open sea and of catching various kinds of fish. He said that four of the thirteen "sea trout" he landed were big enough to supply a table of six people. It is unlikely that this is altogether true, since his mother would not permit sailing. Whatever the real story, it gave Hemingway his first taste of saltwater fishing—and of imaginative writing.

Another example is a letter in 1917 to his grandfather, Anson T. Hemingway, in which he wrote: "The other night I caught three rainbow trout that weighed 6 lb 5½ lb and 3½ lb. respectively. Also a two lb. brook trout in Hortons Bay."

Typical of fishermen relating their latest adventures, he may have then stretched the truth somewhat by adding: "This is the largest catch of trout that has ever been made there."

Since this chapter has been mainly about the origin of "Big Two-Hearted River," I think that including the actual story as the next chapter is fitting. It not only exhibits the unique writing style for which Hemingway became famous, it also demonstrates his skill in weaving complex elements into what at first appears to be a rather simple tale. No one has ever done it better.

2

BIG TWO-HEARTED RIVER

ERNEST HEMINGWAY

I

THE TRAIN WENT ON up the track out of sight, around one of the hills of burnt timber. Nick sat down on the bundle of canvas and bedding the baggage man had pitched out of the door of the baggage car. There was no town, nothing but the rails and the burned-over country. The thirteen saloons that had lined the one street of Seney had not left a trace. The foundations of the Mansion House hotel stuck up above the ground. The stone was chipped and split by the fire. It was all that was left of the town of Seney. Even the surface had been burned off the ground.

Nick looked at the burned-over stretch of hillside, where he had expected to find the scattered houses of the town and then walked down the railroad track to the bridge over the river. The river was there. It swirled against the log spiles of the bridge. Nick looked down into the clear, brown water, colored from the pebbly bottom, and watched the trout keeping themselves steady in the current with wavering fins. As he watched them they changed their positions by quick angles, only to hold steady in the fast water again. Nick watched them a long time.

He watched them holding themselves with their noses into the current, many trout in deep, fast-moving water, slightly distorted as he watched far down through the glassy convex surface of the pool, its surface pushing and swelling smooth against the resistance of the log-driven spiles of the bridge. At the bottom of the pool were the big trout. Nick did not see them at first. Then he saw them at the bottom of the pool, big trout looking to hold themselves on the gravel bottom in a varying mist of gravel and sand, raised in spurts by the current.

Nick looked down into the pool from the bridge. It was a hot day. A kingfisher flew up the stream. It was a long time since Nick had looked into a stream and seen trout. They were very satisfactory. As the shadow of the kingfisher moved up the stream, a big trout shot upstream in a long angle, only his shadow marking the angle, then lost his shadow as he came through the surface of the water, caught the sun, and then, as he went back into the stream under the surface, his shadow seemed to float down the stream with the current, unresisting, to his post under the bridge, where he tightened, facing up into the current.

Nick's heart tightened as the trout moved. He felt all the old feeling.

He turned and looked down the stream. It stretched away, pebbly-bottomed with shallows and big boulders and a deep pool as it curved away around the foot of a bluff.

Nick walked back up the ties to where his pack lay in the cinders beside the railway track. He was happy. He adjusted the pack harness around the bundle, pulling straps tight, slung the pack on his back, got his arms through the shoulder straps and took some of the pull off his shoulders by leaning his forehead against the wide band of the tumpline. Still, it was too heavy. It was much too heavy. He had his leather rod-case in his hand and leaning forward to keep the weight of the pack high on his shoulders he walked along the road that paralleled the railway track, leaving

24

the burned town behind in the heat, and then turned off around a hill with a high, fire-scarred hill on either side onto a road that went back into the country. He walked along the road feeling the ache from the pull of the heavy pack. The road climbed steadily. It was hard work walking uphill. His muscles ached and the day was hot, but Nick felt happy. He felt he had left everything behind, the need for thinking, the need to write, other needs. It was all back of him.

From the time he had gotten down off the train and the baggage man had thrown his pack out of the open car door things had been different. Seney was burned, the country was burned over and changed, but it did not matter. It could not all be burned. He knew that. He hiked along the road, sweating in the sun, climbing to cross the range of hills that separated the railway from the pine plains.

The road ran on, dipping occasionally, but always climbing. Nick went on up. Finally the road, after going parallel to the burnt hillside, reached the top. Nick leaned back against a stump and slipped out of the pack harness. Ahead of him, as far as he could see, was the pine plain. The burned country stopped off at the left with the range of hills. On ahead islands of dark pine trees rose out of the plain. Far off to the left was the line of the river. Nick followed it with his eye and caught glints of the water in the sun.

There was nothing but the pine plain ahead of him, until the far blue hills that marked the Lake Superior height of land. He could hardly see them, faint and far away in the heat-light over the plain. If he looked too steadily they were gone. But if he only half-looked they were there, the far-off hills of the height of land.

Nick sat down against the charred stump and smoked a cigarette. His pack balanced on the top of the stump, harness holding ready, a hollow molded in it from his back. Nick sat smoking, looking out over the country. He did not need to get his map out. He knew where he was from the position of the river.

As he smoked, his legs stretched out in front of him, he noticed a grasshopper walk along the ground and up onto his woolen sock. The grasshopper was black. As he had walked along the road, climbing, he had started many grasshoppers from the dust. They were all black. They were not the big grasshoppers with yellow and black or red and black wings whirring out from their black wing sheathing as they fly up. These were just ordinary hoppers, but all a sooty black in color. Nick had wondered about them as he walked, without really thinking about them. Now, as he watched the black hopper that was nibbling at the wool of his sock with its four-way lip, he realized that they had all turned black from living in the burned-over land. He realized that the fire must have come the year before, but the grasshoppers were all black now. He wondered how long they would stay that way.

Carefully he reached his hand down and took hold of the hopper by the wings. He turned him up, all his legs walking in the air, and looked at his jointed belly. Yes, it was black too, iridescent where the back and head were dusty.

"Go on, hopper," Nick said, speaking out loud for the first time. "Fly away somewhere."

He tossed the grasshopper up into the air and watched him sail away to a charcoal stump across the road.

Nick stood up. He leaned his back against the weight of his pack where it rested upright on the stump and got his arms through the shoulder straps. He stood with the pack on his back on the brow of the hill looking out across the country, toward the distant river and then struck down the hillside away from the road. Underfoot the ground was good walking. Two hundred yards down the hillside the fire line stopped. Then it was sweet fern, growing ankle-high, to walk through, and clumps of jack pines; a long undulating country with frequent rises and descents, sandy underfoot and the country alive again.

Nick kept his direction by the sun. He knew where he wanted to strike the river and he kept on through the pine plain, mounting small rises to see other rises ahead of him and sometimes from the top of a rise a great solid island of pines off to his right or his left. He broke off some sprigs of the heathery sweet fern and put them under his pack straps. The chafing crushed it and he smelled it as he walked.

He was tired and very hot, walking across the uneven, shadeless pine plain. At any time he knew he could strike the river by turning off to his left. It could not be more than a mile away. But he kept on toward the north to hit the river as far upstream as he could go in one day's walking.

For some time as he walked Nick had been in sight of one of the big islands of pine standing out above the rolling high ground he was crossing. He dipped down and then as he came slowly up to the crest of the ridge he turned and made toward the pine trees.

There was no underbrush in the island of pine trees. The trunks of the trees went straight up or slanted toward each other. The trunks were straight and brown without branches. The branches were high above. Some interlocked to make a solid shadow on the brown forest floor. Around the grove of trees was a bare space. It was brown and soft underfoot as Nick walked on it. This was the overlapping of the pine needle floor, extending out beyond the width of the high branches. The trees had grown tall and the branches moved high, leaving in the sun this bare space they had once covered with shadow. Sharp at the edge of this extension of the forest floor commenced the sweet fern.

Nick slipped off his pack and lay down in the shade. He lay on his back and looked up into the pine trees. His neck and back and the small of his back rested as he stretched. The earth felt good against his back. He looked up at the sky, through the branches, and then shut his eyes. He opened them and looked up again. There was a wind high up in the branches. He shut his eyes again and went to sleep.

Nick woke stiff and cramped. The sun was nearly down. His pack was heavy and the straps painful as he lifted it on. He leaned over with the pack on and picked up the leather rod-case and started out from the pine trees across the sweet fern swale, toward the river. He knew it could not be more than a mile.

He came down a hillside covered with stumps into a meadow. At the edge of the meadow flowed the river. Nick was glad to get to the river. He walked upstream through the meadow. His trousers were soaked with the dew as he walked. After the hot day, the dew had come quickly and heavily. The river made no sound. It was too fast and smooth. At the edge of the meadow, before he mounted to a piece of high ground to make camp, Nick looked down the river at the trout rising. They were rising to insects come from the swamp on the other side of the stream when the sun went down. The trout jumped out of water to take them. While Nick walked through the little stretch of meadow alongside the stream, trout had jumped high out of water. Now as he looked down the river, the insects must be settling on the surface, for the trout were feeding steadily all down the stream. As far down the long stretch as he could see, the trout were rising, making circles all down the surface of the water, as though it were starting to rain.

The ground rose, wooded and sandy, to overlook the meadow, the stretch of river and the swamp. Nick dropped his pack and rod-case and looked for a level piece of ground. He was very hungry and he wanted to make his camp before he cooked. Between two jack pines, the ground was quite level. He took the ax out of the pack and chopped out two protecting roots. That leveled a piece of ground large enough to sleep on. He smoothed out the sandy soil with his hand and pulled all the sweet fern bushes by their roots. His hands smelled good from the sweet fern. He smoothed the uprooted earth. He did not want anything making lumps under the blankets. When he had the ground smooth, he spread his three blankets. One he folded double, next to the ground. The other two he spread on top.

With the ax he slit off a bright slab of pine from one of the stumps and split it into pegs for the tent. He wanted them long and solid to hold in the ground. With the tent unpacked and spread on the ground, the pack, leaning against a jack pine, looked much smaller. Nick tied the rope that served the tent for a ridgepole to the trunk of one of the pine trees and pulled the tent up off the ground with the other end of the rope and tied it to the other pine. The tent hung on the rope like a canvas blanket on a clothesline. Nick poked a pole he had cut up under the back peak of the canvas and then made it a tent by pegging out the sides. He pegged the sides out taut and drove the pegs deep, hitting them down into the ground with the flat of the ax until the rope loops were buried and the canvas was drum fight.

Across the open month of the tent Nick fixed cheesecloth to keep out mosquitoes. He crawled inside under the mosquito bar with various things from the pack to put at the head of the bed under the slant of the canvas. Inside the tent the light came through the brown canvas. It smelled pleasantly of canvas. Already there was something mysterious and homelike. Nick was happy as he crawled inside the tent. He had not been unhappy all day. This was different though. Now things were done. There had been this to do. Now it was done. It had been a hard trip. He was very tired. That was done. He had made his camp. He was settled. Nothing could touch him. It was a good place to camp. He was there, in the good place. He was in his home where he had made it. Now he was hungry.

He came out, crawling under the cheesecloth. It was quite dark outside. It was lighter in the tent.

Nick went over to the pack and found, with his fingers, a long nail in a paper sack of nails, in the bottom of the pack. He drove it into the pine tree, holding it close and hitting it gently with the flat of the ax. He hung the pack up on the nail. All his supplies were in the pack. They were off the ground and sheltered now.

Nick was hungry. He did not believe he had ever been hungrier. He opened and emptied a can of pork and beans and a can of spaghetti into the frying pan.

"I've got a right to eat this kind of stuff, if I'm willing to carry it," Nick said. His voice sounded strange in the darkening woods. He did not speak again.

He started a fire with some chunks of pine he got with the ax from a stump. Over the fire he stuck a wire grill, pushing the four legs down into the ground with his boot. Nick put the frying pan on the grill over the flames. He was hungrier. The beans and spaghetti warmed. Nick stirred them and mixed them together. They began to bubble, making little bubbles that rose with difficulty to the surface. There was a good smell. Nick got out a bottle of tomato catchup and cut four slices of bread. The little bubbles were coming faster now. Nick sat down beside the fire and lifted the frying pan off. He poured about half the contents out into the tin plate. It spread slowly on the plate. Nick knew it was too hot. He poured on some tomato catchup. He knew the beans and spaghetti were still too hot. He looked at the fire, then at the tent, he was not going to spoil it all by burning his tongue. For years he had never enjoyed fried bananas because he had never been able to wait for them to cool. His tongue was very sensitive. He was very hungry. Across the river in the swamp, in the almost dark, he saw a mist rising. He looked at the tent once more. All right. He took a full spoonful from the plate.

"Chrise," Nick said, "Geezus Chrise," he said happily.

He ate the whole plateful before he remembered the bread. Nick finished the second plateful with the bread, mopping the plate shiny. He had not eaten since a cup of coffee and a ham sandwich in the station restaurant at St. Ignace. It had been a very fine experience. He had been that hungry before, but had not been able to satisfy it. He could have made camp hours before if he had wanted to. There were plenty of good places to camp on the river. But this was good.

Nick tucked two big chips of pine under the grill. The fire flared up. He had forgotten to get water for the coffee. Out of the pack he got a folding canvas bucket and walked down the hill, across the edge of the meadow, to the stream. The other bank was in the white mist. The grass was wet and cold as he knelt on the bank and dipped the canvas bucket into the stream. It bellied and pulled hard in the current. The water was ice cold. Nick rinsed the bucket and carried it full up to the camp. Up away from the stream it was not so cold.

Nick drove another big nail and hung up the bucket full of water. He dipped the coffeepot half full, put some more chips under the grill onto the fire and put the pot on. He could not remember which way he made coffee. He could remember an argument about it with Hopkins, but not which side he had taken. He decided to bring it to a boil. He remembered now that was Hopkins's way. He had once argued about everything with Hopkins. While he waited for the coffee to boil, he opened a small can of apricots. He liked to open cans. He emptied the can of apricots out into a tin cup. While he watched the coffee on the fire, he drank the juice syrup of the apricots, carefully at first to keep from spilling, then meditatively, sucking the apricots down. They were better than fresh apricots.

The coffee boiled as he watched. The lid came up and coffee and grounds ran down the side of the pot. Nick took it off the grill. It was a triumph for Hopkins. He put sugar in the empty apricot cup and poured some of the coffee out to cool. It was too hot to pour and he used his hat to hold the handle of the coffeepot. He would not let it steep in the pot at all. Not the first cup. It should be straight Hopkins all the way. Hop deserved that. He was a very serious coffee maker. He was the most serious man Nick had ever known. Not heavy, serious. That was a long time ago. Hopkins spoke without moving his lips. He had played polo. He made millions of dollars in Texas. He had borrowed carfare to go to Chicago, when the wire came that his first big well had come in. He could have wired for money. That would have been too slow. They called Hop's girl the Blonde Venus. Hop did not mind because she was not his real girl. Hopkins said very confidently that none of them would make fun of his real girl. He was right. Hopkins went away when the telegram came. That was on the Black River. It took eight days for the telegram to reach him. Hopkins gave away his .22 caliber Colt automatic pistol to Nick. He gave his camera to Bill. It was to remember him always by. They were all going fishing again next summer. The Hop Head was rich. He would get a yacht and they would all cruise along the north shore of Lake Superior. He was excited but serious. They said good-by and all felt bad. It broke up the trip. They never saw Hopkins again. That was a long time ago on the Black River.

Nick drank the coffee, the coffee according to Hopkins. The coffee was bitter. Nick laughed. It made a good ending to the story. His mind was starting to work. He knew he could choke it because he was tired enough. He spilled the coffee out of the pot and shook the grounds loose into the fire. He lit a cigarette and went inside the tent. He took off his shoes and trousers, sitting on the blankets, rolled the shoes up inside the trousers for a pillow and got in between the blankets.

Out through the front of the tent he watched the glow of the fire when the night wind blew on it. It was a quiet night. The swamp was perfectly quiet. Nick stretched under the blanket comfortably. A mosquito hummed close to his ear. Nick sat up and lit a match. The mosquito was on the canvas, over his bead. Nick moved the match quickly up to it. The mosquito made a satisfactory hiss in the flame. The match went out. Nick lay down again under the blankets. He turned on his side and shut his eyes. He was sleepy. He felt sleep coming. He curled up under the blanket and went to sleep.

II

IN THE MORNING THE sun was up and the tent was starting to get hot. Nick crawled out under the mosquito netting stretched across the mouth of the tent to look at the morning. The grass was wet on his hands as he came out. He held his trousers and his shoes in his hands. The sun was just up over the hill. There was the meadow, the river and the swamp. There were birch trees in the green of the swamp on the other side of the river.

The river was clear and smoothly fast in the early morning. Down about two hundred yards were three logs all the way across the stream. They made the water smooth and deep above them. As Nick watched, a mink crossed the river on the logs and went into the swamp. Nick was excited. He was excited by the early morning and the river. He was really too hurried to eat breakfast, but he knew he must. He built a little fire and put on the coffee-pot. While the water was heating in the pot he took an empty bottle and went down over the edge of the high ground to the meadow. The meadow was wet with dew and Nick wanted to catch grasshoppers for bait before the sun dried the grass. He found plenty of good grasshoppers. They were at the base of the grass stems. Sometimes they clung to a grass stem. They were cold and wet with the dew and could not jump until the sun warmed them. Nick picked them up, taking only the medium-sized brown ones, and put them into the bottle. He turned over a log and just under the shelter of the edge were several hundred hoppers. It was a grasshopper lodging house. Nick put about fifty of the medium browns into the bottle. While he was picking up the hoppers the others warmed in the sun and commenced to hop away. They flew when they hopped. At first they made one flight and stayed stiff when they landed, as though they were dead.

Nick knew that by the time he was through with breakfast they would be as lively as ever. Without dew in the grass it would take him all day to catch a bottle full of good grasshoppers and he would have to crush many of them, slamming at them with his hat. He washed his hands at the stream. He was excited to be near it. Then he walked up to the tent. The hoppers were already jumping stiffly in the grass. In the bottle, warmed by the sun, they were jumping in a mass. Nick put in a pine stick as a cork. It plugged the mouth of the bottle enough so the hoppers could not get out, and left plenty of air passage.

He had rolled the log back and knew he could get grasshoppers there every morning.

Nick laid the bottle full of jumping grasshoppers against a pine trunk. Rapidly he mixed some buckwheat flour with water and stirred it smooth, one cup of flour, one cup of water. He put a handful of coffee in the pot and dipped a lump of grease out of a can and slid it sputtering across the hot skillet. On the smoking skillet he poured smoothly the buckwheat batter. It spread like lava, the grease spitting sharply. Around the edges the buckwheat cake began to firm, then brown, then crisp. The surface was bubbling slowly to porousness. Nick pushed under the browned undersurface with a fresh pine chip. He shook the skillet sideways and the cake was loose on the surface. I won't try and flop it, he thought. He slid the chip of clean wood all the way under the cake, and flopped it over onto its face. It sputtered in the pan.

When it was cooked Nick regreased the skillet. He used all the batter. It made another big flapjack and one smaller one.

Nick ate a big flapjack and a smaller one, covered with apple butter. He put apple butter on the third cake, folded it over twice, wrapped it in oiled paper and put it in his shirt pocket. He put the apple butter jar back in the pack and cut bread for two sandwiches.

In the pack he found a big onion. He sliced it in two and peeled the silky outer skin. Then he cut one half into slices and made onion sandwiches. He wrapped them in oiled paper and buttoned them in the other pocket of his khaki shirt. He turned the skillet upside down on the grill, drank the coffee, sweetened and yellow brown with the condensed milk in it, and tidied up the camp. It was a nice little camp.

Nick took his fly rod out of the leather rod-case, jointed it, and shoved the rod-case back into the tent. He put on the reel and threaded the line through the guides. He had to hold it from hand to hand, as he threaded it, or it would slip back through its own weight. It was a heavy, double-tapered fly line. Nick had paid eight dollars for it a long time ago. It was made heavy to lift back in the air and come forward flat and heavy and straight to make it possible to cast a fly which has no weight. Nick opened the aluminum leader box. The leaders were coiled between the damp flannel pads. Nick had wet the pads at the water cooler on the train up to St. Ignace. In the damp pads the gut leaders had softened and Nick unrolled one and tied it by a loop at the end to the heavy fly line. He fastened a hook on the end of the leader. It was a small hook, very thin and springy.

Nick took it from his hook book, sitting with the rod across his lap. He tested the knot and the spring of the rod by pulling the line taut. It was a good feeling. He was careful not to let the hook bite into his finger.

He started down to the stream, holding his rod, the bottle of grasshoppers hung from his neck by a thong tied in half hitches around the neck of the bottle. His landing net hung by a hook from his belt. Over his shoulder was a long flour sack tied at each corner into an ear. The cord went over his shoulder. The sack flapped against his legs.

Nick felt awkward and professionally happy with all his equipment hanging from him. The grasshopper bottle swung against his chest. In his shirt the breast pockets bulged against him with the lunch and his fly book.

He stepped into the stream. It was a shock. His trousers clung tight to his legs. His shoes felt the gravel. The water was a rising cold shock.

Rushing, the current sucked against his legs. Where he stepped in, the water was over his knees. He waded with the current. The gravel slid under his shoes. He looked down at the swirl of water below each leg and tipped up the bottle to get a grasshopper.

The first grasshopper gave a jump in the neck of the bottle and went out into the water. He was sucked under in the whirl by Nick's right leg and came to the surface a little way down stream. He floated rapidly, kicking. In a quick circle, breaking the smooth surface of the water, he disappeared. A trout had taken him.

Another hopper poked his head out of the bottle. His antennae wavered. He was getting his front legs out of the bottle to jump. Nick took him by the head and held him while he threaded the slim hook under his chin, down through his thorax and into the last segments of his abdomen. The grasshopper took hold of the hook with his front feet, spitting tobacco juice on it. Nick dropped him into the water.

Holding the rod in his right hand he let out line against the pull of the grasshopper in the current. He stripped off line from the reel with his left hand and let it run free. He could see the hopper in the little waves of the current. It went out of sight.

There was a tug on the line. Nick pulled against the taut line. It was his first strike. Holding the now living rod across the current, he brought in the line with his left hand. The rod bent in jerks, the trout pumping against the current. Nick knew it was a small one. He lifted the rod straight up in the air. It bowed with the pull.

He saw the trout in the water jerking with his head and body against the shifting tangent of the line in the stream.

Nick took the line in his left hand and pulled the trout, thumping tiredly against the current, to the surface. His back was mottled the clear, water-over-gravel color, his side flashing in the sun. The rod under his right arm, Nick stooped, dipping his right hand into the current. He held the trout, never still, with his moist right hand, while he unhooked the barb from his mouth, then dropped him back into the stream.

He hung unsteadily in the current, then settled to the
bottom beside a stone. Nick reached down his hand to touch
him, his arm to the elbow underwater. The trout was steady in
the moving stream, resting on the gravel, beside a stone. As
Nick's fingers touched him, touched his smooth, cool, underwater feeling, he was gone, gone in a shadow across the bottom
of the stream.

He's all right, Nick thought. He was only tired.

He had wet his hand before he touched the trout, so he would
not disturb the delicate mucus that covered him. If a trout was
touched with a dry hand, a white fungus attacked the unpro-
tected spot. Years before when he had fished crowded streams,
with fly fishermen ahead of him and behind him, Nick had again
and again come on dead trout, furry with white fungus, drifted
against a rock, or floating belly up in some pool. Nick did not like
to fish with other men on the river. Unless they were of your
party, they spoiled it.

He wallowed down the stream, above his knees in the current, through the fifty yards of shallow water above the pile of
logs that crossed the stream. He did not rebait his book and held
it in his hand as he waded. He was certain he could catch small
trout in the shallows, but he did not want them. There would be
no big trout in the shallows this time of day.

Now the water deepened up his thighs sharply and coldly.
Ahead was the smooth dammed-back flood of water above the
logs. The water was smooth and dark; on the left, the lower edge
of the meadow; on the right, the swamp.

Nick leaned back against the current and took a hopper from
the bottle. He threaded the hopper on the hook and spat on him
for good luck. Then he pulled several yards of line from the reel
and tossed the hopper out ahead onto the fast, dark water. It
floated down toward the logs, then the weight of the line pulled
the bait under the surface. Nick held the rod in his right hand,
letting the line run out through his fingers.

There was a long tug. Nick struck and the rod came alive and dangerous, bent double, the line tightening, coming out of water, tightening, all in a heavy, dangerous, steady pull. Nick felt the moment when the leader would break if the strain increased and let the line go.

The reel ratcheted into a mechanical shriek as the line went out in a rush. Too fast. Nick could not check it, the line rushing out, the reel note rising as the line ran out.

With the core of the reel showing, his heart feeling stopped with the excitement, leaning back against the current that mounted icily his thighs, Nick thumbed the reel hard with his left hand. It was awkward getting his thumb inside the fly reel frame.

As he put on pressure the line tightened into sudden hardness and beyond the logs a huge trout went high out of water. As he jumped, Nick lowered the tip of the rod. But he felt, as he dropped the tip to ease the strain, the moment when the strain was too great, the hardness too tight. Of course, the leader had broken. There was no mistaking the feeling when all spring left the line and it became dry and hard. Then it went slack.

His mouth dry, his heart down, Nick reeled in. He had never seen so big a trout. There was a heaviness, a power not to be held, and then the bulk of him, as he jumped. He looked as broad as a salmon.

Nick's hand was shaky. He reeled in slowly. The thrill had been too much. He felt, vaguely, a little sick, as though it would be better to sit down.

The leader had broken where the hook was tied to it. Nick took it in his hand. He thought of the trout somewhere on the bottom, holding himself steady over the gravel, far down below the light, under the logs, with the hook in his jaw. Nick knew the trout's teeth would cut through the snell of the hook. The hook would imbed itself in his jaw. He'd bet the trout was angry. Anything that size would be angry. That was a trout. He had been solidly hooked. Solid as a rock. He felt like a rock, too, before he started off. By God, he was a big one. By God, he was the biggest one I ever heard of.

Nick climbed out onto the meadow and stood, water running down his trousers and out of his shoes, his shoes squlchy. He went over and sat on the logs. He did not want to rush his sensations any.

He wriggled his toes in the water, in his shoes, and got out a cigarette from his breast pocket. He fit it and tossed the match into the fast water below the logs. A tiny trout rose at the match, as it swung around in the fast current. Nick laughed. He would finish the cigarette.

He sat on the logs, smoking, drying in the sun, the sun warm on his back, the river shallow ahead, entering the woods, curving into the woods, shallows, light glittering, big water-smooth rocks, cedars along the bank and white birches, the logs warm in the sun, smooth to sit on, without bark, gray to the touch; slowly the feeling of disappointment left him. It went away slowly, the feeling of disappointment that came sharply after the thrill that made his shoulders ache. It was all right now. His rod lying out on the logs, Nick tied a new hook on the leader, pulling the gut tight until it grimped into itself in a hard knot.

He baited up, then picked up the rod and walked to the far end of the logs to get into the water, where it was not too deep. Under and beyond the logs was a deep pool. Nick walked around the shallow shelf near the swamp shore until he came out on the shallow bed of the stream.

On the left, where the meadow ended and the woods began, a great elm tree was uprooted. Gone over in a storm, it lay back into the woods, its roots clotted with dirt, grass growing in them, rising a solid bank beside the stream. The river cut to the edge of the uprooted tree. From where Nick stood he could see deep channels, like ruts, cut in the shallow bed of the stream by the flow of the current. Pebbly where he stood and pebbly and full of boulders beyond; where it curved near the tree roots, the bed of the stream was marly and between the ruts of deep water green weed fronds swung in the current.

Nick swung the rod back over his shoulder and forward, and the line, curving forward, laid the grasshopper down on one of the deep channels in the weeds. A trout struck and Nick hooked him.

Holding the rod far out toward the uprooted tree and sloshing backward in the current, Nick worked the trout, plunging, the rod bending alive, out of the danger of the weeds into the open river. Holding the rod, pumping alive against the current, Nick brought the trout in. He rushed, but always came, the spring of the rod yielding to the rushes, sometimes jerking underwater, but always bringing him in. Nick eased downstream with the rushes. The rod above his head, he led the trout over the net, then lifted.

The trout hung heavy in the net, mottled trout back and silver sides in the meshes. Nick unhooked him; heavy sides, good to hold, big undershot jaw; and slipped him, heaving and big, sliding, into the long sack that hung from his shoulders in the water.

Nick spread the mouth of the sack against the current and it filled, heavy with water. He held it up, the bottom in the stream, and the water poured out through the sides. Inside at the bottom was the big trout, alive in the water.

Nick moved downstream. The sack out ahead of him, sunk, heavy in the water, pulling from his shoulders.

It was getting hot, the sun hot on the back of his neck.

Nick had one good trout. He did not care about getting many trout. Now the stream was shallow and wide. There were trees along both banks. The trees of the left bank made short shadows on the current in the forenoon sun. Nick knew there were trout in each shadow. In the afternoon, after the sun had crossed toward the hills, the trout would be in the cool shadows on the other side of the stream.

The very biggest ones would lie up close to the bank. You could always pick them up there on the Black. When the sun was down they all moved out into the current. Just when the sun made the water blinding in the glare before it went down, you were liable to strike a big trout anywhere in the current. It was almost impossible to fish then, the surface of the water was blinding as a mirror in the sun. Of course, you could fish upstream, but in a stream like the Black, or this, you had to wallow against the current and in a deep place, the water piled up on you. It was no fun to fish upstream with this much current.

Nick moved along through the shallow stretch, watching the banks for deep holes. A beech tree grew close beside the river, so that the branches hung down into the water. The stream went back in under the leaves. There were always trout in a place like that.

Nick did not care about fishing that hole. He was sure he would get hooked in the branches.

It looked deep, though. He dropped the grasshopper so the current took it underwater, back in under the overhanging branch. The line pulled hard and Nick struck. The trout threshed heavily, half out of water in the leaves and branches. The line was caught. Nick pulled hard and the trout was off. He reeled in and, holding the hook in his hand, walked down the stream.

Ahead, close to the left bank, was a big log. Nick saw it was hollow; pointing up river the current entered it smoothly, only a little ripple spread each side of the log. The water was deepening. The top of the hollow log was gray and dry. It was partly in the shadow.

Nick took the cork out of the grasshopper bottle and a hopper clung to it. He picked him off, hooked him and tossed him out. He held the rod far out so that the hopper on the water moved into the current flowing into the hollow log. Nick lowered the rod and the hopper floated in. There was a heavy strike. Nick swung the rod against the pull. It felt as though he were hooked into the log itself, except for the live feeling,

He tried to force the fish out into the current. It came, heavily.

The line went slack and Nick thought the trout was gone. Then he saw him, very near, in the current, shaking his head, trying to get the hook out. His mouth was clamped shut. He was fighting the hook in the clear flowing current,

Looping in the line with his left hand, Nick swung the rod to make the line taut and tried to lead the trout toward the net, but he was gone, out of sight, the line pumping. Nick fought him against the current, letting him thump in the water against the spring of the rod. He shifted the rod to his left hand, worked the trout upstream, holding his weight, fighting on the rod, and then let him down into the net. He lifted him clear of the water, a heavy half circle in the net, the net dripping, unhooked him and slid him into the sack.

He spread the mouth of the sack and looked down in at the two big trout alive in the water.

Through the deepening water, Nick waded over to the hollow log. He took the sack off, over his head, the trout flopping as it came out of water, and hung it so the trout were deep in the water. Then he pulled himself up on the log and sat, the water from his trousers and boots running down into the stream. He laid his rod down, moved along to the shady end of the log and took the sandwiches out of his pocket. He dipped the sandwiches in the cold water. The current carried away the crumbs. He ate the sandwiches and dipped his hat full of water to drink, the water running out through his hat just ahead of his drinking.

It was cool in the shade, sitting on the log. He took a cigarette out and struck a match to light it. The match sunk into the gray wood, making a tiny furrow. Nick leaned over the side of the log, found a hard place and lit the match. He sat smoking and watching the river.

Ahead the river narrowed and went into a swamp. The river became smooth and deep and the swamp looked solid with cedar trees, their trunks close together, their branches solid. It would

not be possible to walk through a swamp like that. The branches
grew so low. You would have to keep almost level with the
ground to move at all. You could not crash through the branches.
That must be why the animals that lived in swamps were built
the way they were, Nick thought.

He wished he had brought something to read. He felt like
reading. He did not feel like going on into the swamp. He looked
down the river. A big cedar slanted all the way across the stream.
Beyond that the river went into the swamp.

Nick did not want to go in there now. He felt a reaction
against deep wading with the water deepening up under his
armpits, to hook big trout in places impossible to land them.
In the swamp the banks were bare, the big cedars came together
overhead, the sun did not come through, except in patches; in
the fast deep water, in the half light, the fishing would be tragic.
In the swamp fishing was a tragic adventure. Nick did not want
it. He did not want to go down the stream any farther today.

He took out his knife, opened it and stuck it in the log. Then
he pulled up the sack, reached into it and brought out one of the
trout. Holding him near the tail, hard to hold, alive, in his hand,
he whacked him against the log. The trout quivered, rigid. Nick
laid him on the log in the shade and broke the neck of the other
fish the same way. He laid them side by side on the log. They
were fine trout.

Nick cleaned them, slitting them from the vent to the tip of
the jaw. All the insides and the gills and tongue came out in one
piece. They were both males; long gray-white strips of milt,
smooth and clean. All the insides clean and compact, coming out
all together. Nick tossed the offal ashore for the minks to find.

He washed the trout in the stream. When he held them back
up in the water they looked like live fish. Their color was not
gone yet. He washed his hands and dried them on the log. Then
he laid the trout on the sack spread out on the log, rolled them
up in it, tied the bundle and put it in the landing net. His knife

was still standing, blade stuck in the log. He cleaned it on the wood and put it in his pocket.

Nick stood up on the log, holding his rod, the landing net hanging heavy, then stepped into the water and splashed ashore. He climbed the bank and cut up into the woods, toward the high ground. He was going back to camp. He looked back. The river just showed through the trees. There were plenty of days coming when he could fish the swamp.

3

THE LITTLE
REBEL

HE WAS ACTUALLY BORN on July 21, 1899, in Oak Park, Illinois, but the Ernest Miller Hemingway the world eventually came to know as "Papa"—famous author, adventurer, world traveler, and big game fisherman—was really "born" three years later at Walloon Lake in northern Michigan where the family had a summer home. That was where he caught his first fish, which was said to be the biggest of the day.

That's a good way to fire up a beginning fisherman. I know, because my first trip was at about that age, and my dad told me the same thing. For whatever it's worth, I remember it as a sunfish about the size of a silver dollar.

Windemere, the Walloon Lake cottage, provided the Hemingways a remote sanctuary from the city and offered privacy and solitude. Reaching it required taking a steamer from Chicago up nearly the entire length of Lake Michigan to Harbor Springs on Little Traverse Bay, a train to Petosky, and then on to Walloon Lake. The last leg was a rowboat across to the property. Later, a road eliminated that part of the journey.

They had one of the first cottages on the lake's shores in surroundings that were pristine. Today there are homes and other developments virtually all around the shoreline, and while it may still be seen by some as a haven, the total privacy and solitude the Hemingways treasured are long gone.

Up until about the time of his first fishing experience, there was no doubt some confusion in Hemingway's mind about who—or more specifically, what—he was. His mother, Grace, liked to pretend he was a little girl and a twin to his older sister. She dressed them identically and called him her "Dutch dolly." They even were given matching tea sets.

He had shown some signs of rebellion, the most notable of which was calling himself Pawnee Bill after seeing that old Indian fighter's famous Wild West show. He also started mimicking soldiers, cowboys, and other heroic figures, and he tried to sing with a deepened voice in the hope of being seen as a man.

Fishing, however, provided a more promising possibility for escape into the man's world. He immediately became obsessed with this activity, and the daily parade of grubby hands and fishy-smelling clothes that resulted were not compatible with the Dutch-dolly image. Quite the opposite, in fact. A photo taken at age five shows him with a cane pole, oversized creel, and wide-brimmed straw hat. This image almost exactly fits the stereotype of youth popular at the time: a composite drawn from John Greenleaf Whittier's "The Barefoot Boy" and Mark Twain's *Huckleberry Finn*. Many years later, this same sort of image was recaptured by Norman Rockwell in some of his nostalgic illustrations.

Hemingway had his father to thank for rescuing him from the gender puzzle. Dr. Clarence Hemingway was a skilled outdoorsman whose knowledge and interests included not only hunting and fishing, but all of the natural sciences. From the time his son was an infant, he tutored him on bird and animal identification. At two and a half, the young Hemingway knew seventy-three species of birds and their Latin names, early evidence of the remarkable retention that was to serve him so well as a writer. Later he often said: "Remembering is the thing." As any reader of Hemingway knows, he did it very well.

He also learned about rocks and flowers and edible plants, how to build a fire, camp cooking, gun safety, outdoor ethics, taxidermy, how to clean game and fish, survival in the wild, and everything else his father could think of to instill in his young mind. Hemingway was a careful listener, keen observer, and quick to learn. He became a member of the local chapter of the Agassiz Club, a nature study group, when he was five and a half years old. The hikes and other outings of this organization helped satisfy his craving for the outdoors between summers at Windemere.

Clarence Hemingway was his mentor and counselor, determined to give him the best possible instruction, not only about the outdoors, but about life as well. In Michigan he sometimes let his son go with him on calls, providing experiences that would one day be recalled in short stories such as "Indian Camp" and "The Doctor and the Doctor's Wife."

As the size of his family increased, Dr. Hemingway was required to spend more time practicing medicine in Oak Park and less time at Windemere during the summers. But Hemingway remained forever grateful for the gift of knowledge of the outdoors and love of nature that his father gave him, and he treasured the memories of their times together. Years later he recalled them in "Fathers and Sons":

> His father came back to him in the fall of the year, or in the early spring when there had been jacksnipe on the prairie, or when he saw shocks of corn, or when he saw a lake, or if he ever saw a horse and buggy, or when he saw, or heard, wild geese, or in a duck blind; remembering the time an eagle dropped through the whirling snow to strike a canvas-covered decoy, rising, his wings beating, the talons caught in the canvas. His father was with him, suddenly, in deserted orchards

and in new-plowed fields, in thickets, on small hills, or when
going through dead grass, whenever splitting wood or hauling
water, by grist mills, cider mills and dams and always with
open fires.

That's another of the similarities between Hemingway's back-
ground and mine. My father also was determined to teach me
everything about the outdoors and was well qualified to do so.
The difference was that he lacked Dr. Hemingway's patience. He
thought I should be a child prodigy and learn everything
instantly. If I didn't or couldn't, he'd give up in exasperation.
This delayed my learning some of the more sophisticated things
about fishing.

Flycasting, for one. Like Hemingway's, my first fishing gear
was a cane pole. But mine was equipped with a single-action reel
and snake guides. I was eight years old at the time, living in
Sylva, a small town in the mountains of western North Carolina.
The first day I had it I hiked to a nearby creek and caught two
ten-inch trout on crickets in the first pool I fished. I was so
excited that I quit and ran home to show them off.

Later I had a steel telescoping rod that I thought for a while
to be state-of-the-art tackle. I got my first real fly rod, a nine-foot,
split-bamboo wand, by putting it on layaway at a sporting goods
store. I paid for it by delivering newspapers and saving parts of my
allowance. My mother loaned me the last few dollars. She no
doubt wanted me out of my misery.

Much of Hemingway's more advanced trout fishing education
was supplied by a great uncle, Tyler Hancock, who sometimes visited the family at Walloon Lake. Hancock was an expert fly fisherman who taught his nephew casting and angling tactics, as well as
how to tie flies. The two of them would often sneak off from
Windemere and fish some of the small streams in the vicinity.

It's difficult for a young and eager trout fisherman to start out
with flies. I learned early, as did Hemingway, that worms, crickets,

grasshoppers, wasp larvae, and other natural baits pay off extremely well. Fishing bait properly does require a certain degree of skill, but considerably less than it takes to float a dry fly down to a perfect landing at the end of a nine-foot leader.

Hemingway had some Ojibway Indian friends, but apparently none were fishermen. I was luckier, because my dad had an Indian friend named Abe Sanook who took me under his wing and taught me things that improved my success rate remarkably. Abe always accompanied us when we fished the Qualla Reservation at Cherokee, North Carolina, not far from Sylva. I remember that Dad's favorite spot was Raven Fork, a beautiful stream that flows into the reservation from the Great Smoky Mountains National Park.

Abe always fished with a fresh willow pole cut at streamside, and his offering was standard: a gray hackle-yellow wet fly tipped with the larvae of cased caddis. He called it "stickbait." He showed me where to find it, as well as other aquatic nymphs: stone flies, mayflies, Dobson flies, and others. Fished properly with a No. 14 hook and a light leader, nothing is more deadly than these naturals.

My dad, on the other hand, was a purist who used only artificials. I don't think he was even comfortable with spinners. However, bowing to youth's exuberance, he let me do as I pleased, and besides, the kind of tackle I had at that time wasn't designed for fly fishing, anyway.

Summers at Walloon Lake stayed on Hemingway's mind most of the time. In Oak Park there was little opportunity to enjoy the outdoors, and the Agassiz Club activities weren't enough to satisfy him. He made friends with a new boy in town, Lewis Clarahan, and they fished for carp in the Des Plains River. They also caught pickerel and introduced them into Oak Park's water supply, feeding them with goldfish obtained from a local stock pond.

Hemingway's fishing world expanded in the summer of 1906 when he was able to invite one of his Oak Park friends, Harold Sampson, to Walloon Lake for July and August. His father had bought a farm across the lake from Windemere, and the boys erected a tent there and camped out, spending more time there than at Windemere. They soon began hitching rides on lumber wagons to Horton Bay. Wesley Dilworth, the village blacksmith's son, took them fishing in Horton's Creek, a small stream west of Horton Bay that empties into Lake Charlevoix. It was the start of a long association with that particular stream. Hemingway returned to fish it many times during the following eleven years.

Horton Bay is still a small village, and perhaps Hemingway wouldn't find it too different today. He'd be quick, however, to notice the sign by the bridge over Horton's Creek on Highway 630 that proclaims it to be private waters—No Fishing!

I'd like to have tried Horton's Creek. It's reminiscent of some of the narrow, tree-shrouded streams where I first went after brook trout. They're tough to fish, but fun. The only way to do it is to "dabble"—swinging or dropping the bait into every little opening that can be found. Everything goes, including crawling up on likely looking spots on your hands and knees.

Childhood angling experiences might be considered play, but they're much more than that. Fishing provides a youngster with the opportunity to be in contact with nature on a one-on-one basis, not only seeing, but feeling. A camera can capture the view of a golden gauze of haze lying over a pool in a mountain stream, the wings of emerging insects glittering in the muted sunlight above widening rings on the water's surface. But it can't provide the smell of the air or the myriad other sensations of actual experience.

I've seen films of marlin fishing in the Caribbean with brilliant color and spectacular action. Yet I couldn't taste the salt air on my lips, and I didn't feel the electric adrenaline shock that comes when you're sitting on the stern deck of a sport fishing boat and watching a slim, black bill come knifing out of the water.

It's impossible to put into words, but some of us try.

4

EXPLORING THE
COUNTRY

HEMINGWAY'S FIRST VENTURES AWAY from Walloon Lake were to
nearby streams like School's Creek. As he grew older and more
adventurous, he began making weekend excursions, packing up
his camping gear and heading off to explore more distant places.
Much of the surrounding country had been logged, and second
growth created a jungle of underbrush that was hard to walk
through, even on what remained of the old logging roads.

By poking around in this back country Hemingway eventually
found some streams that had stands of big timber nearby where
the forest floor was clear and open. He'd pitch his tent over a bed
made of hemlock and balsam boughs, then go about catching fish
for the evening meal.

Cooking was a pleasure, and he particularly enjoyed preparing
trout, rolling them in corn meal and dropping them into a skillet
crackling with hot bacon grease. That way they came out crisp on
the outside and moist and tender inside. Usually he'd heat a can
of spaghetti or beans to go along with the fish and cut chunks of
rye bread to dip into the bacon grease, polishing the meal off with

canned fruit and hot tea sweetened with condensed milk. Break-fast was usually flapjacks with apple butter or syrup, and lunch was often the onion sandwiches that became a Hemingway trade-mark. The end of the school year in 1915 marked the beginning of the first full-scale adventure. Hemingway was enamored of the vagabond life, and he had made plans for a trip on which it could be experienced. He enlisted his Oak Park pal, Lewis Clarahan, to accompany him, and when school ended, they set out aboard the *Missouri* up Lake Michigan to Frankfort. Once arrived, they began a hiking and fishing trip to Walloon Lake by way of Tra-verse City and Charlevoix.

The trip produced enough fishing opportunities to keep them fed, but it consisted mostly of walking, or riding on the tailgates of wagons. It took them five days to reach Horton Bay, where they arrived tired of walking and weary of a diet of trout and beans. They ate a big meal with Wesley Dilworth's family and went on to Windemere to open the cottage for the summer.

While the first junket wasn't particularly eventful, it was something that fired up Hemingway's desire for more indepen-dence. It also further increased his passion for fishing. That winter he wrote a poem that reflected his great love for the sport:

The Day

I

You may fish all the summer,
You may take the gang of bass
You may catch the muskallonge or
sullen pike
But the time you'll remember
When you've put away your rods
The time you'll remember is The
Day.

52

II

When you started before daybreak,
Mist a-rising from the water;
When your oar strokes sped the
    row boat past the reeds
When the line trailed out behind you
Then a splash! The bass broke water
He had struck it right beside you
Tell me brother
Was not that The Day?

III

When the three of you departed
To fly-fish a brand new trout stream
Wading three abreast against the
    icy flow
And when Al hooked a big one
And Jo one that was larger
And you snagged to a mighty one
And there was not a net among you
Tell me brother
Wasn't that The Day?

IV

When the ice has gripped its rivers
And the lakes are frozen fast
And we're living in the city, trying
    to earn three squares a day
And we're getting kind of grumpy
And the world looks pretty glum
When you get in this condition
And you wish that you were fishin
Stop a minute, Brother Sportsman
Just remember of The Day.

With the summer of 1916 in mind. Hemingway laid plans for a similar trip when the school year ended. Lewis was to be his companion again. This time, though, Hemingway planned for months so they'd be better prepared and would have a more productive route to follow. He had a penchant for details and enjoyed compiling lists of necessary items. The one he prepared for the 1916 trip is in the diary he kept of the adventure, written in an erratic, overlapping backhand style:

2 Blankets	3 lb. Bacon
Cook Kit	Corn Meal
Ax	Watch
2 Reels	Compass
2 Rods	Pedometer
Hooks	Post Cards
Camera	3 Pair sox
Matches	Adhesive tape
Flies	2 maps
Pints Pills	cheese cloth
2 Comb Knife forks	Belt
2 Spoons	Draw 7.00 from Bank
Toilet Paper	Potted meat
Can Opener	german sweet chocolate
Salt and Pepper	Dig worms
Safety Pins	get canvas

This time the hike started at Onekama, south of their point of origin the previous spring. Their initial destination was Bear Creek, near the town of Kaleva. It paid off well, and Hemingway's eighteen-inch trophy established a happy tone for what lay ahead.

Next, they traveled by rail to Walton Junction, then on to Mayfield and the Boardman River. After a couple of days on the Boardman they returned to Walton Junction and took a train to

Kalkaska. From there they hiked to the Rapid River, camping at Rug Pond, a lake created on the river by a power dam. Hemingway said the man who operated the power plant claimed to have twenty-inch trout in the impoundment. They were on the Rapid for nearly two days and fished all of the final night in the rain. They walked back to Kalkaska where they parted company. Lewis headed back to Chicago and Hemingway went on by train to Mancelona and Petosky. He hiked the last miles to Horton Bay, where he spent a couple of days with the Dilworths before returning to Windemere.

In the last part of the diary, Hemingway lists the results of the fishing and a list of expenses for the trip. The latter is interesting in view of today's prices:

		Lew	Ernie
LOG	Mon	1	4
2 Rainbows	Tues	7	3
3 Rainbows	Wed	6	1
3 Rainbows	Thurs	2	3
1 Rainbow	Friday	9	10
Friday night	4 Rainbows	14	16
		—	—
		39	37
	Monday	24	
	Tuesday	8	

ACCOUNT

Bed at Perry's	.75
Chocolate	.15
Bread	.10
Fare to W.J.	1.22
Fare to Mayfield	.25
Supplies at W.J.	.25

Dinner	.30
Paper	.05
Can of Meat	.10
Fare Mayfield to W.J.	.25
Dinner W.J.	.25
Supplies	.20
Fare W.J. to Kalk.	.37
Magazines	.15
Dinner Kalkaska	.20
Sat. Eve. Post	.05
Bananas	.10
Supper at Man.	.15
Fare Man-Pet.	.87

There's no record of how Hemingway decided upon the route he took on the second trip, but it's likely he had some advice in regard to the places he and Lewis fished. He found they were different from the slow-moving, meandering streams he was accustomed to in the area around Walloon Lake. They had faster water than he'd encountered before in his limited experience. In his diary he noted that one river had "a devilish current."

It was nice to discover that all those places they fished remain productive today. Bear Creek is primarily a sandy-bottomed stream with occasional patches of gravel. Between Kelva and Brethren, the part Hemingway and Lewis probably fished, the creek passes through a series of high hills, and there are alternating runs of fast water and long, deep holes. In those days the area was very sparsely populated, so fishing pressure was minimal. The creek has a natural population of brook and rainbow trout, and today it also has tremendous runs of Chinook salmon and steelheads.

The Boardman River, particularly the part between Mayfield and Traverse City, was already quite well known at the time "Ernie and Lew," as they called themselves, made this trip. Throughout its length it's a wild, pretty, freestone river with lots of cedar sweepers that provide good trout cover. It offers good rainbow, brook, and brown trout fishing, especially during Mayfly hatches.

There was once a place called Mayfield Pond off the Boardman where Lynn Halliday, a famous flytier, lived. Halliday, a guide and expert fisherman, invented the Adams, one of the most popular trout flies of all time.

The Rug Pond on the Rapid River that the boys fished washed out many years ago. The dam has been rebuilt, but I doubt that the quality trout it once held are present today. The Rapid River, which flows into Torch Lake, is small in size but has a good population of rainbow and brown trout, as well as seasonal steelhead runs.

At one point in his account of fishing in Bear Creek, Hemingway mentions Lewis catching a grayling, a species which by that time had become rare in Michigan streams. Once these fantastically beautiful fish with flaglike dorsal fins were called "the trout of the pines" and "the trout of the Lower Peninsula." But today the grayling is extinct in Michigan. The last reported catch was in about 1935.

Oddly enough, the brook trout was exclusive to the Upper Peninsula and referred to as an "above the Strait fish." Harold Hinsdill Smedley's *Trout of Michigan*, a detailed history of all of the species, shows that brook trout first showed up in the Lower Peninsula in about 1870 when the decline of the grayling began.

By the time Hemingway fished the Upper Michigan waters, brookies were a dominant species, along with rainbows, which had been first placed in Michigan waters in 1876, and browns, the first stockings of which were in 1889.

Following the hiking trip, Hemingway chose to spend much of the remaining summer of 1916 at Horton Bay. He fished Horton's Creek and spent time with the Dilworths. He also established a closer relationship with Bill and Katy Smith, who lived with their aunt in her summer home there. Katy was nearly twenty-five and Bill twenty-one. Hemingway had known them casually, but that year they became fast friends and the age discrepancies didn't seem to matter. Both were destined to play major roles in his life. In June 1917, Clarence drove Grace and the two boys to Windemere in his Model T Ford touring car and immediately began a regimen of work on the Longfield farm. Hemingway's only relief from the routine was in long weekends spent at Horton Bay, fishing and visiting with Bill and Katy. By comparison, it was a somewhat dull and slow summer. A lot would happen in his life before he spent another one there.

For some time, Hemingway had been making a point of paying particular attention to people and places and making notes of what he observed. Writing was on his mind, and he was seeking subject material. Evidence of this activity exists in an entry in the back of the 1917 trip diary:

GOOD STUFF FOR STORIES AND ESSAYS
1   old couple at Boardman
2   Mancelona—indian girl
3   Bear Creek
4   Rapid River
5   Mancelona, rainy night, tough looking lumberjack, young indian girl, kills self and girl

He had toyed with story ideas before, but now organizing and storing them was becoming increasingly important. In October of that year, he went to work on the *Kansas City Star*, and his writing career was officially launched. The newspaper experience provided some important lessons in writing, the most important of which was brevity. He also gathered more ideas for the stories he hoped to be writing soon.

His tenure at the *Star* was brief. With World War I going on, the mixture of patriotic feeling and desire for adventure led him and a fellow reporter, Ted Brumback, to volunteer for the Red Cross as ambulance drivers.

Hemingway decided that after they drew their final paychecks from the newspaper, a quick trip to Horton Bay to get in some last-minute fishing was in order. Charles Hopkins and Carl Edgar, friends who were waiting to be called by the army and navy, were invited to join them. The foursome stopped overnight in Chicago, then went on to Horton Bay where the Dilworths greeted and fed the happy travelers. Their vacation, however, was of short duration. Soon after they arrived, Hemingway and Ted received a telegram from Red Cross headquarters in St. Louis instructing them to report to New York for their physical examinations within a few days.

◆   ◆   ◆

THE STURGEON, BLACK, AND Pigeon Rivers are in north-central Michigan southeast of Horton Bay in an area that is referred to either as the Pine Barrens or Pigeon River Country. The latter term is more commonly used today because, according to residents, the Pine Barrens represent only a part of Pigeon River Country, not all of it.

There are a couple of interesting similarities among these three rivers. All flow northward into major lake systems in Sheboygan County—the Sturgeon into Burt Lake, the Pigeon into Mullet Lake, and the Black into Black Lake—and all head up in the vicinity of Gaylord. All three rivers also have traditionally been prime trout water, and the beauty of it is that a surprising degree of quality has been maintained; in fact, at least two of them have less fishing pressure now than fifty years ago.

For instance, the little town of Wolverine was once considered the home of the Sturgeon because it was where most people stayed when they came to fish it. The west branch and main branch of the river come together there. In the early days, the only ways to reach Wolverine were on what is now known as old M-27, the main north-south artery through the Pigeon River Country, or by rail. Many fishermen came to spend from a week to a month on the river, and train transportation was the most popular of the choices. Today, however, Interstate 75 bypasses Wolverine, so most people don't know it exists.

The Sturgeon is a deceptive stream with a slick bottom and current velocity of near twenty miles per hour. In this respect, it's treacherous because fishermen unaware of these hazards can be swept off their feet. Other than that, it's a great freestone river with a series of fast runs and deep holes. The river isn't heavily fished anymore, and while the trout opportunity is a far cry from what it was in the years when Hemingway fished it, there are still good populations of rainbows, browns, and brookies throughout its length. The sections of the Sturgeon Hemingway fished were likely those between Wolverine and Indian River or between Gaylord and Vanderbilt. He liked to fish for brookies, so the headwaters were probably his favorite.

The Black River may once have had the finest brook trout fishing in the continental United States. It's still considered to be the best in Michigan, even though siltation from washed-out beaver dams has reduced its productivity considerably. Still, a number of two- to four-pound brookies are taken from it every year, and few anglers turn their noses up at such prospects. This is the stream Hemingway fished and wrote about the most, and one of his favorite stretches of water lies in both directions from the lower bridge on Tin Shanty Bridge Road. Downstream is a spot he mentioned in one of his letters to Bill Smith in 1921, asking if he remembered the day the previous summer when they "hit the big school at that bend down below Chandler's?"

When they made their trips to the Black, the route from Gaylord was on the Old Vanderbilt Road. It's still the same narrow dirt lane, although it's now a side road that branches off the paved Sturgeon Valley Road. Driving down it, I had the feeling it hadn't changed much over the years.

Like the Sturgeon and the Black, the upper reaches of the Pigeon River are in the Pine Barrens east of Gaylord, and the water's characteristics are much the same. It's also a rainbow-brown-brook trout fishery. Hemingway makes little mention of it other than to say he once saw a bear on its banks. Since it lies between the Sturgeon and the Black, chances are he fished it occasionally during the periods he spent roaming and camping in the area. Typically, the party hopscotched from one spot to another.

◆　◆　◆

DAVID RICHEY OF BUCKLEY, a writer and longtime friend, roamed some of Hemingway's old fishing haunts with me and identified others. David was at one time a professional guide, and he's thoroughly familiar with all the trout and salmon waters of Michigan, particularly those in the upper portions of the Lower Peninsula and the Upper Peninsula.

This morning we were standing on a bridge over the Sturgeon, taking a break and soaking up the perfect fall morning. I was watching a succession of golden alder leaves shooting past on the water below me. It was a measure of the swiftness of the current.

"Do you think you've covered about all of Hemingway's waters?" I asked.

"There's no way to know all of the places he might have fished," he said. "Like any fisherman, he'd explore any possible piece of water that might hold a trout. Even though there's no indication that he fished the Bear River, close to Walloon Lake, I suspect that he did. The fact that he hiked to the Minehaha would indicate that he probably tried many other streams that aren't on the record, so to speak."

He turned up his Coke and drained it, then crushed the can and stuck it in his jacket pocket.

"In those days there were many small railroad branch lines," he continued. "And a maze of logging roads provided access to many places that are actually more isolated today than in the past. Hemingway walked, took trains, rode on lumber wagons or in cars—whatever it took to get to fishing waters. I can relate to that, and so can any other dedicated fisherman."

I was listening intently to what he said, but my attention shifted to a hawk that was making slow, lazy circles in the cobalt blue sky overhead.

"Like Hemingway, I spent several summers in my teens in Upper Michigan doing little more than fishing," David said. "I camped in a tent on the Sturgeon near Rondo. That's where I learned to fish for steelheads."

That comment grabbed me. I suddenly realized I didn't recall any mention of these fish in Hemingway's letters or writings. David must have read my mind.

"There were steelheads in some of the Upper Michigan streams in his time, but I doubt that he was aware of them," he said. "Anyway, the runs occur in early spring and late fall, times when he wasn't in the area. Also, the fish weren't well distributed and possibly weren't even present in the waters he fished."

I wondered how he'd class the fishing in this area today. His reply was encouraging. "Of course, nothing will ever match the glory days, but places like Pigeon River Country and parts of the Upper Peninsula are still low-key and offer a better opportunity to discover what yesterday's trout fishing was like than anywhere else."

There aren't many "yesterday" places left. Happily, I've discovered that some of Hemingway's favorites still possess a bit of the old magic.

5

AFTER THE
WAR

FOR HEMINGWAY, THE WAR was brief but brutal. He arrived in
Italy in late May, joined his ambulance unit on June 6, and was
seriously wounded in both legs by a trench mortar on July 8.
Although his time on the battlefield wasn't lengthy, his excep-
tional ability to remember everything he saw and heard and
smelled and experienced supplied him with an enormous amount
of information. He would use it many times and in various ways
in the future.

While hospitalized in Milan, he fell in love with a nurse,
Agnes Kurowsky, who buoyed his spirits during the period
of recuperation. Although she ultimately rejected him, the
romantic interlude resulted in an additional windfall of
story material.

He came home on January 21, 1919, and spent the next four
months recuperating and trying to write. By the time he jour-
neyed to Horton Bay in early June, he had a small store of manuscripts. He stayed for a while with Bill Smith, roaring around the

countryside in Bill's Buick and fishing for big trout in Lake Charlevoix. By the end of the month they had caught six rainbows averaging six pounds apiece. He renamed the fish "the Arditi of the lakes," referring to the Italian shock troops he claimed to have been with during the war.

Hemingway's legs were strong enough by early July for him to make his first fishing trip in two years. The two took Bill's car and headed for the Pine Barrens. In 1919 the area was almost totally uninhabited, dotted with ponds and offering three prime trout rivers within a few miles of each other. He said they went five days without seeing a house or a clearing.

The results weren't disappointing. They camped at several places on the Black and caught more trout than they could eat at each location. Twice Bill caught two trout at once, using a dropper rig and a fly-grasshopper combination. On the final day the pair caught a total of sixty-four fish then headed home triumphantly, sporting a week's growth of beard and a generous number of mosquito bites.

Hemingway wasn't satisfied for long. He next invited his friends Howell Jenkins and Larry Barnett, another veteran of the ambulance service, to join him and Bill on a return trip to the Black. They were scheduled to come up in August.

"Bill and I have a complete camping outfit for 4 men," he wrote Howell. "Tents, blankets, cooking utensils, camp grate and so forth. Where we will go is the Pine Barrens and camp on the Black River. It is wild as the devil and the most wonderful trout fishing you can imagine. All clear—no brush, and the trout are in schools."

Everything came off as planned. The weather was fine and the fish were cooperative. They "caught and ate many beautiful trout," Hemingway reported. As before, nobody shaved, and they were a shaggy-looking lot when they pulled into Horton Bay.

After Howell Jenkins returned home, he received an update on Hemingway's exploits. The letter is dated September 15:

Yesterday Bill and Kate and Jock and I and the Madam [Bill and Kate's aunt] went over to the Black and it rained like hell so we only got 23. Jock 8—I nine—Bill 4—Kate 2. They weren't biting because of the rain. But we had some Darbs. 11½ of the inches. We were over at the Black once before and rated 40. Bill had one that broke his leader on the stricture. Bill claims he was 3 or 4 of the pounds. A Hooper [grasshopper] is an easy article to lay hold of now that today is the last day of the season.

Hemingway's emphasis on his total of fish suggests his highly competitive nature, a characteristic that became more intense as he grew older. It existed in everything he did. While at times it was useful as a driving force, it was just as often a disadvantage. He could be a poor loser, and sometimes he offended or alienated people with this sour trait. A related quality, evident early on, was his fierce desire for leadership. For good or bad, he often pushed both attributes to the limit.

The final excursion of the summer was the September trip to the Fox with Al and Jock. He had no way to know that it would be responsible for launching his legendary literary career.

◆　　◆　　◆

HEMINGWAY STAYED ONLY BRIEFLY in Oak Park upon his return in October. He was anxious to do some serious writing, but he knew it couldn't be accomplished in that atmosphere. Instead, he went back north to Petosky, rented a room in a boarding house, and started pounding out stories. He also became well known in the town for his gripping tales of his time with the Arditi. One such performance, a talk before the Ladies' Aid Society, resulted in an offer from Harriet Connable, the wife of a wealthy Toronto businessman, Ralph Connable, head of the Canadian branch of F. W. Woolworth Company. Mrs. Connable offered Hemingway the job of acting as her crippled son's companion while she, her husband, and daughter were in Palm Beach for the winter. He liked the idea immediately and accepted. The son was only a year younger than Hemingway, and besides, it meant visiting new territory.

The city's major newspaper, the *Toronto Star*, which published both daily and weekly editions, immediately caught his attention. Within a week of his arrival, he asked Mr. Connable about the possibility of doing some reporting or writing for it. Connable introduced him to a friend in the advertising department, who in turn introduced him to a couple of the reporters. He wasn't offered a job, but after seeing him hanging around the newsroom for a couple of weeks, the editor gave him space rates in the weekly bulldog section.

It was the chance he'd been waiting for. He hadn't been able to market any of the stories he'd written, and this offer allowed him at least to see his work in print and make a few extra dollars.

Since he wasn't an employee of the paper and on assignment, he could select his own subject material. As a result, he turned in features on a wide variety of topics. Not surprisingly, he wrote about fishing several times, the first of which was in the April 10, 1920, edition, a piece titled "Trout Fishing." Following that were "Trout-Fishing Hints," April 24, 1920; "The Best Rainbow Trout Fishing," August 28, 1920; and "Indoor Fishing," November 20, 1920. He also did a couple of other pieces that referred to his Upper Michigan experiences: "Camping Out," June 26, 1920; and "Ted's Skeeters," August 7, 1920.

The agreement with the Connables expired in May, and Hemingway was eager to get back to Michigan for the summer. Since he was a freelancer with the newspaper, he could continue to submit features by mail. He made a quick stopover in Oak Park then went on to Horton Bay to meet Bill Smith. Hemingway was nurturing a plan whereby he and Ted Brumbeck would ship out for the Far East in the fall. He visualized Ted signing on as an able seaman, with himself as a stoker. That was as far as the idea got. In the meantime, another group venture was being plotted. He was using all of his persuasive powers to make sure everyone joined in.

In a letter to Jim Gamble, a friend from the war days in Italy, he painted an optimistic picture:

> And let me tell you about the Rainbow fishing. I don't know whether you are a fisherman or not. But you might be a rank hater of the sport and you would like this kind of fishing. Across the little Bay from where we would live is a point. And a little trout river comes into the Bay and makes a channel past this point. There is an old quay alongside and it is from there that we fish. And this is the manner of the fishing. We paddle over across the Bay and stop at this old lumber dock, just level with the water. And from the dock we run out about four or five lines into the channel. These are baited with whole skinned perch which is dropped into the channel and sinks to the bottom. The lines are run out and then we put a weight on the butt of the rod they are run out from and set the click on the reel and wait. Do you get the scene. All the rods, sticking out over the side, the clicks set, and the lines running way out into the channel. Then if it is night, we have a campfire on the point and sit around and yarn and smoke or if it is daytime we loaf around and read and await results. And these are the results. A reel goes screeeeeeech, the tip of the rod jerks underwater, you run down and grab it up and thumb the reel and then out in the lake a big rainbow shoots up into the air. And then the fight. And Jim, those trout can fight. And I've never taken one under three pounds out of the Bay and they run as high as fifteen. The biggest I ever took was nine and seven ounces. And you always get a strike. A night's fishing would average three of the big trout. Though I have taken as high as seven. It is the best rainbow trout fishing in America. Just this one Bay and the only thing you can take them on is a skinned perch. And nobody knows it but us. People come down and troll all day for them from Charlevoix and never get a strike. While we will be taking them all day. An Indian taught it to me.
>
> And they break water a dozen times and when you have one you have a regular fish. And it is the most comfortable

kind of fishing I have ever found. When we feel like doing regular trout fishing, we can fish any one of the half hundred good streams for brook trout. But it's a great life up there just lazing around the old point and always having a line out or so for rainbow. There are trips in the car and runs around Little Traverse Bay to the old Indian missions and some beautiful trips. And Jim we are going to have a wonderful gang up there. Bill who I told you of is a wonder. Then there is Carl Edgar, a Princeton man of the same easy going humorous type as Bill Horne. Who reads fairy tales and swims and fishes when anyone else wants to. He's been an artillery officer during the late unpleasantness. Carl's coming up in July. Charles Hopkins, a newspaperman and general good scout and mighty fisherman and loafer is coming up whenever I write him that everything is ready. Hop is the only one who takes his fishing seriously.

Hemingway's "big plan" didn't work out. Both Gamble and another friend, Johnny Miller, declined the invitation. So did Bill Horne and Hopkins. Bill and Katy Smith were at Horton Bay, as usual, and a few other pals—Howell Jenkins, Jock Pentecost, and Ted Brumback—were around for part of the time.

They fished the Black mostly. On one trip with Brumback, Jenkins, and a new friend named Dick Smale, Hemingway tells of everyone curling up around the campfire and listening to Brumback play the mandolin and himself reading aloud from *Lord Dunsany's Wonder Tales*. One day Bill Smith and his aunt and uncle, the Charleses, came to visit, and they caught fifty trout for them to take home.

When October rolled around, Hemingway departed with Bill, Kate, and Mrs. Charles for Chicago. The next time he returned, a dramatic change would be about to take place in his life.

Getting a job in Chicago proved to be more difficult than he had anticipated, even with the help of friends. In the meantime, he met Hadley Richardson, a former classmate of Katy Smith's, who had come from St. Louis to visit. She stayed for three weeks, and in that period a romance developed between them that was continued by mail. After Hemingway got a job with a monthly magazine, he was able to visit her. That was in March. When he went back again in May, the marriage plans were settled, but he had certain misgivings. He knew marriage was going to bring an end to the kind of life he had been leading, mainly the carefree summers of fishing. He described his feelings in a letter to Bill Smith:

> Doubt if I get up this summer—Jo Eezus, sometimes get thinking about the Sturgeon and Black during the nocturnal and damn near go cuckoo—Haven't got the Odgar [Carl Edgar] attitude on that. May have to give it up for something I want more—but that doesn't keep me from loving it with everything I have. Dats de way tings are. Guy loves a couple or three streams all his life and loves 'em better than anything in the world—falls in love with a girl and the goddam streams can dry up for all he cares. Only the hell of it is that all that country has as bad a hold on me as ever—there's as much of a pull this spring as there ever was—and you know how it's always been—just don't think about it at all daytimes, but at night it comes and ruins me—and I can't go.

He was extremely restless, and when warm weather arrived, he began sleeping on the apartment roof. He'd lie awake, looking up at the moon and stars, pondering what lay ahead in life.

The wedding was set for September 3 at a country church near Windemere. Hemingway managed to arrive on the Sunday before the ceremony, and he set out with Howell Jenkins and Charles Hopkins for a final fishing fling on the Sturgeon River.

It was near the end of the trout season, and their success was less than spectacular. Still, it was a time for Hemingway to savor his last remaining days of freedom and independence. He thought of all of his favorite streams and of the good times he and his companions had on them. No doubt he envisioned coming back someday, but in truth it was his last visit to these treasured waters. He would return again only in memory or through the adventures of his alter ego, Nick Adams.

PART 2

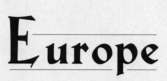

Europe

6

DATELINE, PARIS

HEMINGWAY ARRIVED IN PARIS in December 1921 as the *Toronto Star*'s first foreign correspondent. The terms were generous considering the economics of the time. When on assignment, he would receive seventy-five dollars a week plus expenses. For every unassigned piece he would be paid a penny a word. He also was invited to continue to submit material for the *Star* weekly.

He hit the ground running. When the *Leopoldina*, the ship he and Hadley were traveling on, made a four-hour stop at Vigo, Spain, Hemingway's observation of the fishermen resulted in one of his earliest dispatches to the *Star*: "Tuna Fishing in Spain."

During the next three years he covered events in France, Spain, Switzerland, Germany, Italy, Turkey, Bulgaria, and Greece for the *Star*, assignments which allowed him to discover angling opportunities throughout Europe. Once identified, he followed up on them on holidays with Hadley in Spain, Germany, Austria, Italy, and Switzerland.

Oddly enough, France offered the least potential. In fact, Jack Hemingway, the writer's oldest son, says his father never fished in that country. In his book *Misadventures of a Fly Fisherman*, he relates what apparently was the extent of his involvement at that time:

> My first experience of fishing—which was to become a lifelong passion—was strictly as a spectator sport. There was always fishing of some sort going on along the quaisides and embankments of the Seine. Whenever I went there with Papa to visit the bookstalls, or with Tonton, my nurse's husband, a retired soldier who worked in the French civil service, we would stop and watch the fishermen of the Seine. They were, and still are, a breed that's unique. These men with weatherbeaten faces and shabby clothes, wielding their long bamboo poles with goose-quill bobbers seemed as rooted in the landscape as the ancient trees. . . .
>
> You need to watch longer now to see an angler on the Seine catch a fish than you did in those bygone times. Some in the old days were successful enough to be able to sell their catches of whitebait to the small specialty restaurants which deep-fried them for finger eating. They were a great treat and a great favorite of my father's and mine.

Hemingway's only published comment on the subject appeared in a dispatch to the *Star* weekly, "Trout Fishing in Europe," in November 1923. It contained a humorous sketch about an American fishing for trout near Deauville on a private stream owned by a French financier. After two hours of fishing, one trout had been caught: a five-and-a-half-inch specimen with peculiar black spots on its sides. The American said he didn't think the trout was healthy, to which the financier replied: "Healthy? You don't think he's healthy? That lovely trout! Why, he's a wonder. Did you see the terrific fight he made before I netted him?"

And in regard to the spots: "Those spots? Oh, absolutely nothing. Perhaps worms. All our trout here have them at this season. But do not be afraid of that, Monsieur Zshones. Wait until you taste this beautiful trout for breakfast!"

The incident may be fictitious or tongue-in-cheek, but it sheds light on the opinion Hemingway had of French trout fishing. In the same dispatch, he had good things to say about some other places:

The real trout fishing of Europe is in Spain, Germany and Switzerland. Spain has probably the best fishing of all in Galacia. But the Germans and the Swiss are right behind.

In Germany the great difficulty is to get permission to fish. All the fishing water is rented by the year to individuals. If you want to fish you have first to get permission of the man who has rented the fishing. Then you go back to the township and get a permission, and then you finally get the permission of the owner of the land.

If you have two weeks to fish, it will probably take about all of it to get these different permissions. A much easier way is simply to carry a rod with you and fish when you see a good stream. If anyone complains, begin handing out marks. If the complaints keep up, keep handing out marks. If this policy is pursued far enough the complaints will eventually cease and you will be allowed to continue fishing.

If, on the other hand, your supply of marks runs out before the complaints cease, you will probably go either to jail or the hospital. It is a good plan, on this account, to have a dollar bill secreted somewhere in your clothes. Produce the bill. It is 10 to 1 your assailant will fall to his knees in an attitude of extreme thanksgiving and on arising break all existing records to the nearest, deepest and wooliest German hand-knitted sock, the South German's savings bank.

The Hemingways essentially followed this plan, and they managed to catch some nice trout. Because of the hassle involved, however, they never came back. With excellent options at other places, it wasn't worth the trouble.

Fishing in France is even more restrictive today, with most of the streams and rivers owned by resorts and private interests. The chance of a tourist being successful freelancing through the region as Hemingway did would be zero or less.

7

SWITZERLAND

GEORGE JAQUET HAS JUST revealed himself, and I am grateful for
the revelation. He has been smiling while I assembled my pack
rod, attached the reel, and threaded the line through the guides,
and he nodded in approval when I showed him a box of dry flies.
The trouble is that it seems to be more a polite smile than an
interested one.

"When I was younger," he says, "I used to fish with flies. It was
fun, but not very productive. I learned that I could catch more
with bait. Grubs are now my favorite 'fly.' Also, I like to fish in
the high lakes. There are more trout, and bigger ones.

"You see, my fishing time is limited, so I go where I can get
the best results. I like to cook, and I want trout for the table."

He is more candid than some trout fishermen I know, and I
don't disdain his angling methods. Fishing natural baits is an art
form separate from fly fishing, and in some cases there's just as
much expertise required.

We're standing beside a long, straight, green-flanked aisle of
water that I'd view as nothing more than a ditch if it weren't for

the location and what it represents. As I look out across the grain fields and up at the Alps that frame the broad valley, I think about what Hemingway wrote about it:

> In the afternoon a breeze blows up the Rhone Valley from Lake Geneva. Then you fish upstream with the breeze at your back, the sun on the back of your neck, the tall white mountains on both sides of the green valley and the fly dropping very fine and far off on the surface and under the edge of the banks of the little stream, called the Rhone canal, that is barely a yard wide, and flows swiftly and still.
>
> Once I caught a trout that way. He must have been surprised at the strange fly and probably struck from bravado, but the hook set and he jumped into the air twice and zigged nobly back and forth and toward every patch of weed at the current bottom until I slid him up the side of the bank.
>
> He was such a fine trout that I had to keep unwrapping him to take a look and finally the day got so hot that I sat under a pine tree on the bank of the stream and unwrapped the trout entirely and ate a paper-bag full of cherries I had and read the trout-dampened Daily Mail.

It is not the Rhone Canal that we are preparing to fish, but the Stockalper, its nearly identical twin. The two canals bracket the Rhone River less than a kilometer apart. Looking up the river, the Rhone Canal is on the left and the Stockalper Canal on the right. We planned to fish the Rhone Canal, but circumstances make the Stockalper a better choice. A prolonged dry spell has created unusually low water, and the level is down more than two feet in both canals. Under normal conditions, the Rhone is very narrow; now it is even slimmer. The Stockalper is broader and offers more fishing room. Besides, it was Hemingway's favorite of the two.

It seems logical that the Rhone River would also be an option, but one look at it reveals why it isn't. The river is roily with a greenish-chalky color. George says this is caused by silt

The Stockalper Canal, slow and glassy, was Hemingway's favorite Swiss trout water.

washed down from the valley and that it's even worse in the spring and early summer when snow-melt water is added. He tells me almost nobody fishes it, which comes as no surprise.

George's method of fishing intrigues me. He is using a "frame" instead of a reel, a rectangular wooden device on which the line is stored. It's somewhat clumsy looking and seems out of place used with a modern fiberglass rod. For whatever reason, however, it's his preference. I notice that he plays out and retrieves line with it quite efficiently.

It isn't the best time of the day for fishing. George couldn't get away until late in the morning, and then we stopped at a charming restaurant in the little town of Villeneuve. There were prints of Impressionist paintings on the wall—Renoir and Monet—and we ate morel mushrooms on toast and filet

George Jaquet's "frame," which he uses instead of a reel.

mignon and wonderful French fries and forgot about fishing for the moment. Noon came and went, and now as my first cast drops a Royal Wulff on the water it is close to two o'clock. For that matter, I realize that late August isn't the best time of the year, either. That adds one more plausible excuse in case of a strike-out.

I discover there is one other nagging problem. Somewhere upstream they are mowing the banks of the canal, and the grass floating on the water makes drifting a fly more than a couple of feet impossible. It is touch and go: drop the fly on the surface, watch it carefully, then pick it up when it encounters the first bit of grass. A trout has little time to make up its mind. It turns out that nothing happens, but the majestic mountains and sparkling environment easily erase any sense of disappointment. Frankly, I can think of no time in the past when I enjoyed being skunked more.

George fared better. His "frame-work" results in three trout, two browns and one rainbow, and he politely avoids any comment on my zero score.

"It is a wonder I caught any," he says. "Spring is the time to fish the canals. The big trout and salmon come up from Lake Geneva, and they are hungry and eager to strike.

80

"I do not know this from personal experience, only through what I have been told. You see," he adds, "in springtime is when I am on the lakes!"

◆　　◆　　◆

AFTER HIS ARRIVAL IN Paris, Hemingway was slow in getting started on work for the *Star*. Instead, he and Hadley were barely settled in their apartment before he decided they should go to Switzerland and learn to ski.

They left for a two-week vacation at Chamby, a little village in the mountains above Montreaux, a beautiful small city on the east end of Switzerland's Lake Geneva. Someone had told them about a chalet there near the ski slopes. The Gangwisch pension was run by a German-Swiss family, and the Hemingways rented a double room there for less than five dollars a day, meals included.

Jaquet and I compare a couple of trout fished from the Stockalper Canal. Both were caught by him; I was shut out.

The accommodations and food exceeded their best expectations. The room was spotless and comfortable, with a big window they could open at night to let in the fresh, cold winter air. In the mornings, Madame Gangwisch would come into their room, close the windows, and build a roaring fire in the porcelain stove. When the room warmed up, she would bring the Hemingways breakfast in bed.

Hemingway boasted of the great food in a letter to Katy Dos Passos, telling her of meals of soup, roast beef, creamed cauliflower, fried potatoes, and blueberries with whipped cream. As usual, his appetite was enormous for both the food and the local wines and beer.

They learned to ski and felt the exhilaration of riding a bobsled or a luge down the icy mountain roads. These things and other experiences were included in dispatches he sent to the *Star* on his return to Paris, and

The Gangwisch Pension, where Hemingway and Hadley stayed when they vacationed at Chambry, Switzerland, in 1922. Today it is a private residence.

Three nice trout from the Stockalper Canal, which flows into Lake Geneva near Montreaux. Trout and salmon migrate seasonally into both the Stockalper Canal and its twin, the Rhone Canal.

much later in reminiscences contained in *A Moveable Feast*. He was gathering material in the area, too, that would later appear in short stories. As always, his curiosity was insatiable, and he was constantly talking to people, asking questions, and taking notes.

He was also thinking past the winter season. Once the snow was gone, the mountains promised green meadows and rushing trout streams and hikes. When they returned to Paris, these idylls were on his mind, and he couldn't wait to get back.

He followed up on this urge in May when an assignment from the *Star* to go to the Soviet Union failed to materialize. He made contact with an old pal from the war, an Englishman named Eric "Chink" Dorman-Smith, who agreed to meet them in Chamby for some trout fishing and mountain climbing. The trio had great

fun scaling local peaks and sliding down the slopes on the
remaining snow crust.

They also had the opportunity to enjoy the wonderful ambi-
ence of Montreaux, the "Swiss Riviera," where despite its location at the foot of the Alps, winter temperatures seldom drop
below forty degrees Fahrenheit. Even more remarkable, today
there are palm trees growing in the magnificent gardens that
border the six-kilometer promenade along Lake Geneva.

At first, Hemingway fished only the Stockalper Canal, since
the Rhone Canal was still swollen with snow water. Hadley and
Chink accompanied him on the train to Aigle then waited across
from the station at a cafe which had a galloping golden horse on
the roof. They read and drank beer, hearing the humming of bees
in a great wisteria vine that grew over the arbor. This became an
almost daily ritual. Days later, when the Rhone Canal cleared, he
was able to try his luck there.

Hemingway also wanted to walk across the St. Bernard Pass
into Italy so he could show Hadley the places of his wartime
adventures. It was a long trek that proved to be a miserable experience for Hadley. When they finally arrived in Aosta, she was
exhausted and had badly blistered feet. She recovered in Milan
and accompanied Hemingway on his nostalgic tour to the place
he was wounded and the hospital where he recuperated.

Memories of Chamby may have been on their minds on the
train back to Paris, and possibly the idea of returning in the
winter. But coming events would change such plans.

8

ITALY

"YES, I KNEW HEMINGWAY," the old man says. "I once fished with him." He is sitting straight and dignified as he waits for his interpreter, Andrea Ghiretti, to translate his words into English for me. Once the translation is completed, he begins talking again, this time at greater length.

"He does not want you to use his name," Andrea explains. "He says that many people come to Cortina to interview him about the old days, and sometimes his words are not quoted correctly."

He is obviously a very proud man, and truth is important to him. I agree to honor his request, but with some regret, knowing that a photograph will also be forbidden. Still, I'm eager to hear what he has to say. Assured that everything is understood, the story continues to unfold.

"I am eighty-seven years old. When Hemingway first came to Cortina in 1923, I was nineteen and working as a driver in public transportation. I drove people to and from the hotels and the train station. At that time, all of them were English or American. Later the Germans started coming.

"Maybe I saw Hemingway in those days, but I do not remember it. He was not famous then, so I would have perceived him as just another traveler. My experience with him was in 1949. He was staying at the Concordia Parc Hotel. It was the best-known hotel in the town at that time, and it is still operated by the Appolonio family."

He stops for a moment as if to further gather his thoughts. It is late afternoon, and a brassy, glancing light tints the cobblestones in the street outside the office in which we are meeting. A low buzz of pedestrian conversation waxes and wanes with their passing. Over the roof of a building I can see the towering peak of one of the chalk-white mountains that surround the town.

"The concierge at the hotel came to me and said there was an American staying there who wanted to go fishing. There were few fishermen in Cortina then, and he thought I would know the best places to go.

"I speak only Italian, so I contacted a friend, Count Federico Kechler, to ask if he would accompany me on a fishing trip with this American. Kechler spoke excellent English."

He pauses again, and a smile comes to his face. When he again speaks to Andrea, he is chuckling softly. "We went to a beautiful lake in the Anterselva Valley between Dobiacco and Brunico, about seventy-five kilometers from Cortina.

"We had been fishing for only about fifteen minutes when Hemingway disappeared. There was a bar nearby, and that's where we found him. He was drinking and talking with the other patrons. Hemingway stayed there all day while Kechler and I fished.

"It was the only time I was with him. Hemingway and Kechler became good friends and fished together many times after that. He told Kechler that the way to catch big trout in the lakes was to first catch a small trout and skin it. Then you put it on a big hook, cast it out and wait for action. Kechler did this and caught a trout that weighed a kilo and a half."

Cortina, Italy, is nestled among the magnificent Dolomite Mountains. Hemingway first visited Cortina with Hadley in 1923; he came back with Mary in 1948 and 1950.

It was a trick Hemingway had learned at Walloon Lake many years before. The old man shifts in his chair and stares out the window. The look of merriment is gone from his eyes.

"The people of Cortina were saddened to learn of Hemingway's death," he said. "He was a kind and convivial man, and he had many friends here."

◆   ◆   ◆

IN FEBRUARY 1923, HEMINGWAY and Hadley came to Rapallo, Italy, to visit Ezra Pound in what he considered to be his special hideaway on the Mediterranean coast. All went well for a while, but eventually they became disenchanted with the humid sea-level atmosphere that seemed quite dull and boring in comparison to the exhilarating environment at Chamby. When the Pounds set off in early March on a walking tour of the region, the Hemingways declined to join them. Instead, they boarded a train for Cortina de Ampezzo, a small town in northeastern Italy.

The beautiful, crystal-clear Boite River flows through Cortina.

Cortina was much like Switzerland, with great skiing opportunities, rugged snow-capped peaks all around, and a friendly population. The town is nestled in the Dolomites, spectacular mountains formed eons ago by the uplift of an ancient sea. Some of the spirelike crests tower to altitudes of more than thirty-two hundred meters, providing many sheer and thrilling ski runs. When the Hemingways arrived, the main season was over, so there were plenty of inexpensive hotel rooms available. They stayed at the Hotel Bellevue on the Corsica Italia, which at that time was quite popular with the American and English visitors.

Not long after they arrived, the *Star* assigned Hemingway to cover a political flare-up in the Ruhr region of Germany. Hadley had recently found that she was pregnant, and when Hemingway departed for Germany, he left her behind in Cortina, lonely and feeling miserable.

When he returned in April, the snow was gone and the conditions were better for fishing than skiing. He tried several of the nearby streams, one of which probably served as the setting for "Out of Season," a story about a young man who is encouraged by a disreputable local character to fish a stream that is not legally open. The wife goes along but is repulsed by the guide and eventually decides to return to town. The trip is aborted when the young man discovers he has forgotten his lead sinkers. He is relieved that he doesn't have to violate the law. The question remains as to whether this experience was fact or fiction for Hemingway. Chances are that it was a little of both.

When Hemingway came back again twenty-five years later in the fall of 1948, he was a famous figure whom the Italians treated like a returning hero. His home base was then Havana, Cuba. He and Mary, his fourth wife, checked in at the Concordia Park Hotel. It was not long afterward that he met Count Kechler, who was willing to take him fishing. They made short trips to some of the nearby mountain lakes, but they mainly fished in local streams.

The most accessible of these was the crystal-clear Boite, which passes through Cortina. It is a lovely stream with a bed of

white dolomite, which causes the water to take on a greenish hue in the deeper runs and pools. Hemingway remembered it from the 1920s when there was virtually no fishing

In 1950, Hemingway stayed here, at the Hotel de la Poste in Cortina.

pressure, and he and Kechler found the situation still much the same. Cortina's appeal in those days was primarily to skiers. The area's other attractions had not yet been promoted.

Cortina hasn't lost its appeal as a mountain paradise, but it has outgrown the "small village" category. It was the site of the Winter Olympics in 1956, and the resulting focus of attention boosted the population from four thousand to eight thousand. Town officials have halted further development, hoping to preserve its charm and natural beauty. It is an outstanding location and deserves such protection.

From an angler's standpoint, it's still a desirable spot. Fishing remains good in the Boite, even though its once all-wild population of trout is now supplemented by stocking. Also, people are restricted to fishing only four days a week, with a daily limit of five.

In October 1948 the Hemingways went back to Milan. While there, Hemingway wrote an article for *Holiday* magazine, "The Great Blue River," which contains the nucleus for his later Nobel Prize–winning *The Old Man and the Sea*. Also during the stay in Milan, Hemingway went partridge shooting with Count Carlo Kechler, brother of Federico. It was on this trip that he met the young Adriana Ivancich, who would become the model for the heroine in his next novel.

The Hemingways left this note in the 1950 ledger for the Hotel de la Poste.

The Hemingways decided to winter in Cortina. They returned in December and rented the Villa Aprile, a chalet on the outskirts of town. This time a series of misfortunes marred their stay. Mary broke an ankle while skiing, and not long after, Hemingway came down with a severe cold. The final blow came when a small scratch on his eye led to a serious infection. With limited medical facilities in Cortina, the local doctors sent him to Padua for hospitalization and treatment.

Venice was the next destination, where Harry's Bar, the Gritti Palace Hotel, and the general winter atmosphere combined to inspire the idea for a short story about duck shooting in the nearby lagoons. The more he thought about it, the larger it grew in his mind, and on the voyage back to Havana, he realized it had become a novel.

Back at the *Finca Vigia* in Havana in May, he plunged into the effort and had it nearly completed in five months. As it progressed, he considered several titles, among them *The New-Slain Knight* and *The Things That I Know*. He finally decided upon *Across the River and into the Trees*, a slightly altered version of Stonewall Jackson's last words, as the most appropriate choice.

Hemingway and Mary had another European vacation planned, so he decided to complete the work during their travels. In November they flew to New York to meet with his publisher, Charles Scribner, and also to finalize an agreement for serialization of the book in *Cosmopolitan* magazine. Hemingway worked on the last chapters during his return crossing on the *Ile de France*. Once in Paris and established in the Ritz Hotel, he spurted for the finish.

Declaring himself a "winner again," Hemingway was in a holiday mood when he, Mary, and Virginia and Peter Viertel left Paris on Christmas Eve. Hemingway had rented a large Packard car and driver and planned a leisurely tour through the south of France, along the Riviera coast, and over to Venice. After weeks of socializing with friends in Nice and Venice, Mary said that she wanted to see Cortina again. In early February they checked into the Hotel de la Poste for the weekend and ended up staying two weeks. One week after arriving, Hemingway developed a skin infection much like the one he had had the year before. As a result, the trip ended on an unpleasant note.

It was Hemingway's last visit to the delightful Italian village he had enjoyed at different times over a period of twenty-seven years.

9

SPAIN

VICTOR URDIROZ, MANAGER OF Hostal Burguete, is all smiles as he shows me "the piano that Hemingway played," an ancient upright with chipped and yellowed keys tucked away in a hall off the main lobby. He lifts the top lid under which a tattered picture of Hemingway, in his fifties, is pasted. My guess is that it was clipped from a Spanish magazine, probably a feature on him at the bullfights.

Yet that isn't all Victor has to offer. He steps out of the room briefly and returns with a pencil portrait of his grandmother, Marieta Apat, who operated the hotel at the time Hemingway and Hadley made their first visit to the tiny village of Burguete in 1924.

"She has been dead since 1970," he explains. "She was ninety-three years old." He poses with the portrait, so I realize a photo opportunity is being provided. I take one shot and he quickly assumes a different pose. I take another.

"I will show you the room in which they stayed," he says, "although the picture of the Virgin that hung in it has been

Victor Urdiroz, manager of the Hostal Burguete, stands beside "the piano that Hemingway played." He holds a pencil drawing of his grandmother, who was the manager of the hotel at the time Hemingway visited the Basque village.

moved to another room. Otherwise, it is still much the same."

This isn't exactly a recommendation. Hadley found the accommodations extremely Spartan. The room was unheated, with two hard beds, a clothes stand, and a wash basin. The chill was such that when they went down to the dining room for dinner, she played the piano to warm her fingers. In other words, *a* Hemingway played the piano, not *the* Hemingway.

The next day I learn that the tiny town has a taxi. I talk to the owner, a jolly Basque named Pedro Tellechea, whom I find to be part historian, part philosopher, and part entertainer. He agrees to drive me to the Irati and show me the places pertinent to the Hemingway legend.

I find that they are numerous. In fact, at nearly every turn of the river, there is a spot where Pedro believes Hemingway stood, fished, ate, or slept. Along the way we also stop at a place where a steady stream of water flows from a pipe into a concrete trough.

"This was here when Hemingway visited," he said, "and he drank from this spring. The water is very pure." We drink from the pure waters of "the Hemingway spring." Further on I also view the small tavern where he ate lunch and maybe spent the night. It's closed now.

◆　　◆　　◆

Burguete, a quaint basque town in the Spanish Pyrenees with a single narrow street lined with centuries-old houses, might have forever remained encased in a soft cocoon of anonymity if Hemingway hadn't written about it. Even so, the impact has been light. Unlike some of the places he immortalized in his writings, virtually no visible evidence of his presence remains. There are no postcards, T-shirts, or trinkets. His name is familiar, but mostly to the older residents.

Pedro Tellechea shows me a spring at which Hemingway is alleged to have stopped for water.

A battered sign near Arive identifies the river that Hemingway sought out during his 1923 visit to Spain.

It's fairly easy to understand why. Pamplona, forty kilometers to the south, was the focus of Hemingway's attention, and trips to Burguete and the Irati River were incidental. Pamplona, a center-piece in *The Sun Also Rises* and *Death in the Afternoon*, became the major Hemingway shrine in Spain. Besides, there are no bull-fights or wild revelry, nor are there bulls running down the street in Burguete.

Hemingway, constantly on the lookout for new fishing adventures, heard of the Irati River on his first trip to Spain in 1923. The following year he organized a fishing trip to the river at the end of the festival in Pamplona. Bill and Sally Bird and Robert McAlmon left early and took the bus to Burguete. Hem-ingway and Hadley followed a couple of days later. Soon after-ward they were joined by Chink Dorman-Smith, John Dos Passos, and George O'Neil, who planned a two-week walking trek in the Pyrenees.

Hemingway described the trip to the river in a letter to William B. Smith in December 1924:

96

This summer Chink and Dos Passos and George O'Neil (Dave O'Neil's kid from St. Louis—) started to walk across the Spanish face of the Pyrenees and I walked up a ways with them and hit a little town on the Irati and got a little tight at lunch and a Spaniard offered to show me the biggest trout on the Irati that had lived in the same hole for 3 years now and it was where the women wash the clothes in about 10 ft. of water and the bastard would weigh 16 lbs. easy. I tried him with everything and finally poked him with my rod to see if he was real and he damned near knocked the rod out of my hand. If you could find what corresponds to muddlers in the Irati you could get trout up to any size. You get plenty of medium sized ones. Hash and I got 7 out of one hole and they were jumping all the time.

The Irati River, flanked by the Pyrenees, flows through numerous Basque villages that appear unchanged by time.

97

An earlier account of the experience appears in a November 1924 letter to Howell Jenkins:

> There is swell fishing. Like the Black when we first hit it. The wildest damn country in the Spanish Pyrenees in from Roncevaux. The Irati river. We hit it this summer. You leave the car at Burguete and go in fifteen miles by foot. Even the mules pass out on the trail. It is there where they fought the Carlist wars. We butchered them this summer. Big trout. Hadley caught six in less than an hour out of one whole [sic] where they were jumping the falls. Water ice cold and virgin forests, never seen an ax. Enormous beech forests and high up, Pines.

The account is somewhat exaggerated. Departing from Burguete there are three primitive roads, or trails, to what locals call the Valley of the Fabrica, an old munitions factory on the Regata Legarza. The Legarza is a tributary that joins the Irati at the point where the river swings eastward, not far from the tiny village of Orbaiceta.

The distances vary slightly, the most lengthy being about seven and a half miles, so it could have been a fifteen-mile round trip. Also, Burguete is 898 meters above sea level, and at no place do any of the trails exceed 1,188 meters. The steepest ascent is just over 100 meters, hardly enough to exhaust a mule. Hemingway may have been thinking about the road from Pamplona to Burguete, which does make a very steep, switchback climb into the Pyrenees.

There's an easier way to the Irati, though. It's less than six miles by road from Burguete to Arive, and even though it wasn't paved in 1924, it was certainly an available option. Local residents say it has been there for centuries.

Although the first visit to the Irati satisfied Hemingway's wildest expectations, the second, in 1925, shattered them. He

had boasted of the river to Bill Smith and Don Stewart, two of
his old fishing pals, and invited them to fish it along with him
and Hadley. They made the trip from Pamplona to Burguete on
an old two-tiered bus filled with Basques who had ample wine
to share with them. They arrived drunk but happy. It didn't take
long for the mood to change. The proprietress of Hostal Burguete told them loggers had been cutting the forests alongside
the Irati and floating the logs down the river. The dams had
been broken down and the pools filled with trash and debris.
They tried, anyway. Bill Smith had brought along a box of the
flies he and Hemingway had always found dependable in Michigan waters—Royal Coachmans, McGintys, and Yellow Sallys—
but nothing worked. They quit flies and tried worms and
grasshoppers, then finally abandoned the Irati for some of the
smaller streams in the Valley de la Fabrica. Still, after four days
fishing, they had had no success. It was Hemingway's last fishing
trip on the Irati.

He made many more trips to Spain, however, and in June
1931 he wrote John Dos Passos about the wonderful town of
Barco de Avila in the Sierra de Gredos west of Madrid:

> We live on 3.00 a day the two of us. Now is the time to buy
> anything if anybody had money. . . . Killed a wolf there while
> we were there. Bear paw nailed to door of the church—good
> trout—River Tormes then flows down to Salamanca—wild
> goats. Eat better than Botins—same dishes—swell big *clean*
> rooms—no chinchas [bugs]—damned intelligent—all people
> nice—old banner of Garibaldi from 1st Republic at Verbena of
> San Juan—all for 8 pesetas a day.

The loggers' scars on the slopes of the Pyrenees that border
the Irati have long been healed. The forests have returned, and
the river valley is probably much like it was when Hemingway
first saw it. The houses and other buildings in the tiny Basque

villages along the river have a timeless appearance, as if centuries come and go and leave no marks. The blacktop road is the only noticeable concession.

The fishing is good, and the Irati is again a producer of big trout. And perhaps after a few bottles of wine, one of the local anglers might be persuaded to show off the current Irati monster fish.

There's usually one in every river.

10

AUSTRIA

"THAT IS THE PLACE where Hemingway came to watch the wood-cutters work," Max Salzgeber says. He is pointing to a gap in the tree line on the upper side of a broad green pasture rising sharply to our left. "The logs were brought there after they were cut. Then they were dragged or rolled down to the road and loaded onto wagons. As you can see, it has been a long time since trees were cut at this place. Today the forests are managed and the harvests carefully regulated."

I'm grateful for the pause in our stiff uphill climb. We've come more than four kilometers up the Gauertal Valley, and even though it is a pleasantly cool September day I'm damp with perspiration. This morning when I left the hotel in Schruns, I could see my breath. Now I'd be more comfortable in shorts and a T-shirt.

Visiting this little-known "Hemingway location" is the main reason for the hike, but I think Max is equally interested in having me experience the charm and beauty of this Alpine valley

This vista of a high Alpine valley is similar to that which Hemingway saw when he watched some woodcutters at work.

in western Austria not many kilometers from the Swiss border. He has been the director of tourism for the village of Tschagguns for many years and knows the Montafon region intimately, yet I have the sense that the Gauertal is his favorite place.

Truthfully, although Max may not realize it, he hasn't had my full attention. Almost since the start of our walk we've been traveling parallel to the Rasafeibach, a gin-clear, tumbling mountain stream that is hauntingly reminiscent of the one in the Balsam Mountains of western North Carolina where I caught my first rainbow. The memory came rushing back the instant I saw it, and I'm caught in a strange kind of time warp: hiking along in the Austrian Alps and recalling the thrill of landing a ten-inch trout many years ago in a place thousands of miles away. I am thinking, too, of how I cooked it over the campfire and that no trout since has ever tasted nearly as good.

The Hotel Taube in Schruns, Austria, has changed little since Hemingway and Hadley first stayed here in 1924.

Half an hour later Max and I are sitting at a table outside the Gauertalhaus, a guest house just off the trail. As we enjoy a snack of sauerkase, a local specialty cheese, along with rye bread and apple juice, I tell him how badly I want to fish this beautiful stream.

"There is no possibility," he says. "It is private water, and patrolled against intruders. But it is well stocked with fish, and those who own it have very good success."

Well, it isn't the first time that I've been unable to fish a tantalizing trout stream for one reason or another, and it probably won't be the last. I don't feel deprived, though. Yesterday, Jakober Simon, a local expert, guided me on the Ill River where I caught and released more than half a dozen brown trout. Tomorrow, the Litz and Suggadin are possible choices.

◆　　◆　　◆

This plague on the front of the Hotel Taube commemorates visits by Hemingway in 1925 and 1926. It is slightly inaccurate in that the Hemingways actually arrived on December 20, 1924.

HEMINGWAY AND HADLEY LOVED Chamby, but in 1924 their financial resources had dwindled to the point where they could not afford another winter interlude in the Alps. This problem was solved when Bertram Hartmann, an American painter, told them of the little village of Schruns in the Austrian Vorarlberg. Hartmann said that there was excellent skiing, but most important, runaway inflation in the country would make their cost of living very affordable. The figure he quoted was two million kronen a week, which Hemingway discovered amounted to $28.50 for himself, Hadley, and their son, Bumby. He immediately sent a check to Paul Nels, owner of the Hotel Taube, reserving two rooms for December 20th.

The Hemingways arrived a few days before Christmas to discover weather that was more like September. The Montafon Valley was still green, and cows were grazing in the pastures. Although they had come to ski, the existing conditions diverted Hemingway's mind to fishing, at least for a while. In one chapter in *A Moveable Feast* titled "There Is Never Any End to Paris," he recalls their arrival in Schruns:

104

We went to Schruns in the Vorarlberg in Austria. After going through Switzerland you came to the Austrian border at Feldkirch. The train went through Liechtenstein and stopped at Bludenz where there was a small branch line that ran along a pebbly trout river through a valley of farms and forests to Schruns, which was a sunny market town with sawmills, stores, inns and a good, year-round hotel called the Taube where we lived.

At the time, Hemingway told Hadley he could feel the trout swimming in the river, and it's likely thoughts of past autumns in Michigan—of the Black and Boardman and Sturgeon—came flooding back.

There were additional reminders. In Schruns, two beautiful trout streams beckoned to him: the Litz River that flows through the town, and the Ill River between Schruns and the adjacent village of Tschagguns. That wasn't all. Because he was restless and anxious for snowfall, he began burning his pent-up energy by exploring the nearby mountains. On his hike up the Gauertal to watch the wood cutters, he saw the Rasafeibach, which must have elicited more memories.

The register of the Hotel Taube for March 1926 lists the three Hemingways, Gerald and Sara Murphy, and John Dos Passos as guests.

Max Salzgeber and I enjoy our lunch at a guest house in the mountains as we follow Hemingway's tracks up the Gauertal.

Here were sparkling streams in magnificent settings, yet the most important element was absent: opportunity. It was winter and the fishing season was closed. The situation was look-but-don't-touch, and it didn't change. He went back to Paris in March, well before angling was again legal.

Much the same thing happened in the winter of 1925–26, except that there was lots of snow when he arrived. He could ski daily, and it's doubtful that trout fishing entered his mind. He was still working on *The Sun Also Rises* and in the process of trying to change publishers in New York.

Something else entered his mind, however, and it was to have an enormous impact on his life. Just before Christmas, Pauline Pfeiffer, an acquaintance from Paris, came to spend the holidays with them. Her appearance marked the beginning of the end of his marriage to Hadley.

106

Flowing through Schruns, the Ill River caught Hemingway's attention, but he never had an opportunity to fish it.

He made a quick trip to New York, then stopped over in Paris for a romantic rendezvous with Pauline before returning to Austria. Soon afterward, John Dos Passos and Gerald and Sara Murphy came to visit. They all skied around Schruns, then moved briefly to the Posthotel Rossle at Gaschurn, higher up the Montafon Valley to try other slopes.

The situation between Hemingway and Hadley remained calm, and if she suspected anything, it wasn't apparent. But the undercurrent of deceit was there, and secretly Hemingway was very much disturbed.

He never came back to fish the streams of the Montafon that undoubtedly registered in his mind. Perhaps Schruns, like Chamby, held too many haunting memories. Whatever the reason, they qualify as "Papa's waters" to me. Standing hip-deep in the icy Ill River watching a dry fly drift through a long riffle, I recognized the paradox of the situation: if he hadn't found them, I wouldn't have, either.

PART 3

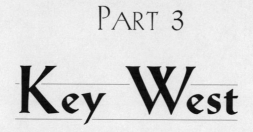

Key West

11

KEY WEST

FROM ONE OF THE living room windows in the Hemingway Suite in the La Concha Hotel in Key West there is a long view eastward up Duval Street. It is a peaceful vista in the pearly light of early morning. The street is empty of traffic and tourists, and I find myself trying to visualize how it must have looked in the old days before the town was transformed from a sleepy, laid-back village into a bustling destination point for what sometimes seems to be about half the population of the eastern United States.

In a couple of hours, but before the tours begin, I will go to the Hemingway House and browse around. It has been more than twenty years since I first visited it, yet the memories are still vivid in my mind. At that time I spent most of an afternoon talking with its owner, the late Bernice Dickson, who, along with her husband, had been friends with Hemingway and his second wife, Pauline. When the tours were over for the day, she let me swim in the famous saltwater pool. Now her niece, Sylvia Robards, manager of the property, has invited me to come by an hour before the daily deluge of tourists begins.

Yesterday I made a before-hours visit to Sloppy Joe's, when the bartender was its only other occupant. The bar has quite a history. Named after its owner, Josie Russell, it was a "box-like elbow bar" at the foot of Duval Street when Hemingway first patronized it in 1928. Shortly after Prohibition ended, it was moved to 428 Greene Street. Then in 1937 it moved to its present Duval Street location. The walls are covered with Hemingway photos, posters, fishing rods, and other memorabilia. It's a genuine shrine, because even though Hemingway frequented all the Sloppy Joe's locations over the years, it is the present one with which he is most closely associated. The house, the bar— those are the obvious reminders of Hemingway's years in Key West. Much of Duval Street is manufactured nostalgia and reminiscence, which is okay, but in a search for the authentic, it's the out-of-the-way that has potential.

A couple of days ago I was walking along a back street, a lane bright with red and purple bougainvillea and modest weathered homes. Ahead of me, on the sidewalk, were a hen and several little chicks scrutinizing the ground and occasionally pecking at what appeared to be bits of grass and leaves. A soft breeze offset the heat of the noonday sun, and as I stood there, I could hear strains of Latin music and the sound of laughter coming from a house set well back from the street. Was this what Key West was like sixty years ago?

Later that day, still in the Conch community, I stopped in a working-class bar several blocks off the main thoroughfare. Again, music, but this time loud and lively, intermixed with a constant buzz of conversation that was a melange of languages and dialects. It was a rich mixture, and I hung around, knowing that these feelings and this atmosphere were what I was looking for.

Conch, incidentally, doesn't refer to a race of people, but to a kind of people. Or better still, a way of life. Conchs are natives of the Keys, descendants of people who long ago populated this strand of jewel-like tropical islands strung out below mainland

Florida like an unclasped necklace. The term is more loosely applied today. Some outsiders who are longtime residents of the Keys take on the characteristics inherent in the Conch culture and are accepted into the clan.

◆   ◆   ◆

HEMINGWAY CAME TO KEY West in 1928 with the hope of finding a quiet place to relax and write. He had spent nearly seven years as an expatriate in Europe and enjoyed limited success, but the trauma of his divorce from Hadley and his discovery that Pauline was pregnant made the idea of returning to America both desirable and sensible.

The choice of Key West resulted from the glowing accounts given him of it by another expatriate, John Dos Passos, the peripatetic writer who had once hitchhiked through the region. Dos Passos described the 120-mile journey down through the Keys on the Florida East Coast Railroad as "something seen in a dream." He insisted that it was the ideal place for "Ole Hem to dry out his bones." In his 1966 book, *The Best Times,* Dos Passos remembered what the island was like when he first visited it in the early 1920s:

> In those days Key West really was an island. It was a coaling station. There was shipping in the harbor. The air smelt of the Gulf Stream. . . . [Cayo Hueso, as half the people called it, was linked by car ferries with Havana.] Cigar factories had attracted a part Cuban, part Spanish population. . . . The Englishspeaking population was made up of railroad men, old Florida settlers, a few descendants of New Englanders from the days when it was a whaling port, and fishermen from such allwhite settlements as Spanish Wells in the Bahamas.

These cultural influences were reflected in the architecture of the town. Key West houses represented Greek and Gothic revivals with the addition of Bahamian-style open-air porches and long, overhanging eaves typical of West Indies homes. The widow's walks and high peaked roofs were pure New England, and the filigrees, trellises, and balustrades were copied from New Orleans, although at Key West they were done in wood rather than wrought iron.

By the time Hemingway arrived, however, things weren't quite as rosy as Dos Passos's description suggested. Key West had been in a state of decline since the end of World War I. The once thriving cigar industry was dying, and the Key West navy yard was all but abandoned. Both the Mallory Steamship Line and a Florida east-coast sea freight business had closed down. Various other commercial enterprises were either defunct or only barely surviving. In addition, the population had shrunk from twenty-six thousand to ten thousand. Things would get even worse with the coming of the Depression.

Yet Hemingway was not threatened by the deteriorating economic conditions. Although he liked to complain occasionally to friends about "being broke," the threat of poverty wasn't hovering over him. Pauline had money of her own, provided by her father, a successful Arkansas businessman who owned a cotton gin and large parcels of land. In addition, she was a favorite of her Uncle Gus, who owned Sloan's Liniment and Richard Hudnut Perfumes, and who eventually bought them the house on Whitehead Street. Uncle Gus liked the burly, hard-driving Hemingway, and the feeling was mutual. He was to continue to be a sort of guardian angel in their lives.

Both Hemingway and Pauline found Key West appealing and well suited for their needs. The tropical climate was welcome after a cold Parisian winter, and the pace was slow and easy. Not only that, but Hemingway was quick to see that it was a fisherman's paradise. It was this factor more than anything else that would hold him there for what were to be the happiest ten years of his life.

It was also a very productive decade. During the Key West years he wrote all or parts of some of his most important works, including *A Farewell to Arms*, *Death in the Afternoon*, *Winner Take Nothing*, *To Have and Have Not*, *Green Hills of Africa*, "The Short Happy Life of Francis Macomber," "The Snows of Kilimanjaro," *The Fifth Column*, *The Spanish Earth*, and the initial portion of *For Whom the Bell Tolls*. He also produced many articles for *Esquire*, *Colliers*, *True*, *Look*, and other magazines.

A new Model A Ford roadster, a homecoming gift from Uncle Gus, was supposed to be at Key West upon their arrival, but shipment was delayed. Until it came, Hemingway fished off the steamship dock. A little over a week later he was mobile and making daily excursions up U.S. 1, fishing off wharves, docks, and bridges. He was using basic tackle and bait and enjoying the wide variety of species. His excitement and enthusiasm grew daily. All he needed was someone to "show him the ropes."

One of the famous six-toed cats snoozes on a table in the yard of the Hemingway House on Whitehead Street in Key West.

He was fortunate in finding an excellent mentor. Within a couple of weeks he was introduced to Charles Thompson, a local merchant and avid angler. The two hit it off right away, and they started making daily trips to nearby in-shore spots in Thompson's eighteen-foot motorboat. They caught the usual mixture of species that inhabit these waters, but Thompson also got them into some tarpon action. This was Hemingway's first experience with truly big fish, and it excited him tremendously. He wrote about it in an April 28, 1928, letter to his editor at Scribner's, Maxwell Perkins:

> Have been catching tarpon, barracuda, jack, red snappers, etc. Caught the biggest tarpon they've had down here so far this season. Sixty-three pounds. The really big ones are just starting to come in. Also a barracuda on a fly rod. Great quantities of sharks, whip rays and other vermin. We sell the fish we get on the market (the edible ones) and get enough to buy gas and bait. Have been living on fish too.

Thompson was teaching Hemingway valuable lessons about tackle, terminal rigs, lures, and bait preparation, as well as the identification of the various species they caught. Hemingway, who had fished only in fresh water, found that saltwater angling was a vastly different world that posed new and formidable challenges. His desire to learn was boundless, and Thompson quickly became aware of his highly competitive nature and bulldog tenacity. Their daily sessions soon became contests. Hemingway gained confidence with each trip, and his skills improved steadily. It was only a matter of time until he would consider himself an expert.

Because of the responsibility of running a store, Thompson could fish only in the late afternoons, but this worked perfectly with Hemingway's schedule. He was proceeding on the manuscript of *A Farewell to Arms*, which he had begun in Paris, and he devoted his mornings to writing. He wanted to complete the novel so it could be included in Scribner's 1929 publications list.

Hemingway's next new fishing acquaintance was destined to play an important role in his adventures for a long time to come. Captain Eddie "Bra" Saunders, a forty-two-year-old sun-creased Conch, was one of the most respected of Key West's charter boat captains. A white Bahamian from Green Turtle Key, he was familiar with and comfortable in all the waters from Cuba to the Rebecca Shoals off the Tortugas. He was also an experienced Gulf Stream fisherman, and Hemingway had a burning desire to fish that mysterious azure current.

Hemingway and Thompson hired Captain Bra to take them on a weekend trip to the Marquesas Keys, some thirty miles west of Key West and only a few miles from the Gulf Stream. The Marquesas, a necklace of keys consisting of one large island and five small ones, form an atoll. The lake in the center provides a safe haven for docking as well as a fine place to dive for crawfish and conch and to catch yellowtails and other prime food fish for the larder.

Thirty miles beyond the Marquesas are the Dry Tortugas, another cluster of small keys that were one of Hemingway's favorite locations for settling in when he was fishing the blue water. Historic Fort Jefferson, on Garden Key, was originally intended to protect America's southernmost waters and also serve as a coaling station. Construction was begun in 1846, but in 1876 the project was abandoned. In the interim, it served as a Federal prison during the Civil War. What remained was a huge brick structure that occupied almost all of the island.

The Marquesas Keys excursion went well. Hemingway and Thompson caught lots of fish, and with Captain Bra's coaching, Hemingway landed his first sailfish. The feat marked the onset of a lifelong obsession with big-game fishing, particularly billfish. Impatient for knowledge, Hemingway spent every spare minute on the trip pumping Captain Bra for all sorts of fishing information, from catching to cooking.

Hemingway always found great delight in discovering new places. In Key West—as had been the case earlier in Michigan,

Spain, Switzerland, Austria, and Italy—he wanted to share the benefits of his newfound paradise with his friends. With nearly half of the novel completed, he decided to celebrate by putting together a so-called Mob of some of his old pals. He sent letters of invitation to artists Mike Strater and Waldo Pierce; Bill Smith, his friend from boyhood days; and writers John Dos Passos and Archibald MacLeish.

Once they arrived and were installed in the Overseas Hotel, they were joined by some of the new acquaintances Hemingway had made in Key West: Thompson; Captain Bra and his half brother, Burge; Josie Russell, owner of Sloppy Joe's bar; Hamilton Adams and Jakie Key, charter boat captains; Earl Adams, a local newspaperman; and J. B. Sullivan, a machinist. The Mob quickly became notorious in all of the local bars and restaurants.

Hemingway held fairly steadily to his routine of writing in the mornings. In the afternoons, he joined the Mob for drinking, swimming in the navy yard harbor, or bottom fishing in the shallows for snappers and Jewfish. The crowning event was a trip to the Dry Tortugas on Captain Bra's charter boat, with Hemingway, Strater, MacLeish, Pierce, and Dos Passos on board. Thompson followed in his motorboat, accompanied by Burge. To accommodate Thompson's restricted schedule, they agreed to stop at the Marquesas Keys for the weekend, then proceed from there when he had to return to Key West.

The Marquesas provided a setting as remote from civilization as most of the visitors had ever seen, and they exulted in the surroundings. The tarpon fishing was great, and Waldo Pierce caught one that weighed 138½ pounds. They pulled out at the end of the weekend and were in fine spirits when Captain Bra tied up at the Fort Jefferson docks in the Tortugas.

The group alternated between the fort and nearby Loggerhead Key, fishing for tarpon around the islands and going out daily to troll in the Gulf Stream. Hemingway lost a giant sailfish, and Pierce set a new record for hooked-and-lost tarpon.

The most significant result of the trip was something Hemingway observed at the time but which would appear only much
later in print. As usual, he had been cataloging everything he saw
or experienced, and one of his observations was that Captain
Bra's gnarled and weathered hands had a tendency to stiffen
badly as the day progressed. "Rheumatism" was the mundane
diagnosis, but the picture of those hands and the tired face of the
Conch fisherman were indelibly etched into his mind. The first
hint of what that image would create showed up in a paragraph of
a 1936 *Esquire* article titled "On the Blue Water":

> Another time an old man fishing alone in a skiff out of
> Cabañas hooked a great marlin that, on the heavy sashcord
> handline, pulled the skiff far out to sea. Two days later the old
> man was picked up by fishermen sixty miles to the eastward,
> the head and forward part of the marlin lashed alongside. What
> was left of the fish, less than half, weighed eight hundred
> pounds. The old man had stayed with him a day, a night, a day
> and another night while the fish swam deep and pulled the
> boat. When he had come up the old man had pulled the boat
> up on him and harpooned him. Lashed alongside the sharks
> had hit him and the old man had fought out alone in the Gulf
> Stream in a skiff, clubbing them, stabbing at them, lunging at
> them with an oar until he was exhausted and the sharks had
> eaten all they could hold. He was crying in the boat when the
> fishermen picked him up, half crazy from his loss, and the
> sharks were still circling the boat.

Thirty years later, in 1952, the image emerged again, this
time as the novel *The Old Man and the Sea*. Within days after the
Mob dispersed and headed home, Hemingway and Pauline
packed up the Model A Ford and began the fourteen-hundred-
mile trip to Piggot, Arkansas. The baby was due in June, and it
was agreed that Kansas City provided the best hospital in the
area. The first leg of the journey was the most tedious. The

Key West is renowned as the "end of the world in North America," and it is also the terminus of U.S. Highway 1.

Florida City–Key West highway link still wasn't complete. There were two major water gaps remaining that had to be crossed by ferries. They left No Name Key at 9 A.M. and arrived in Florida City near sunset.

They had been in Key West for only seven weeks, but that was sufficient time for Hemingway to put down the roots that would make him want to return. It offered everything he required: a place where he could combine work and play; a group of fine companions; and a slow, lazy way of life in an idyllic atmosphere. Best of all, there was unlimited fishing opportunity that he had only begun to explore.

Key West was sometimes referred to as "the end of the world in North America," and not always in a complimentary sense. For Hemingway, however, Key West provided the perfect situation, whether or not he knew it when he first arrived. Dos Passos had been right.

12

AT HOME

THE GULF STREAM IS an enchantress. Like the Sirens of Greek mythology, its seductive powers are irresistible. Yet unlike those ancient vamps whose voices lured seafarers to their doom, the effect of the stream's dazzling beauty and great mystique is to snare anglers into a lifelong love affair.

I live inland myself, and even though over the years I've fished the Gulf Stream from North Carolina's Outer Banks to the Bahamas, there is always too much time between rendezvous. I know I'll never get enough of it. But then again, maybe nobody can.

Part of what causes the stream to be unique is that it is a separate entity, a powerful force plowing its way through the Atlantic Ocean as it follows a predestined course. The current is generated in the Gulf of Mexico and from there moves around the tip of Florida and makes its way up the eastern U.S. coast. Next, it crosses the North Atlantic, then turns south and parallels the coast of Europe until its energy is finally exhausted. Along the way, the stream's slow, serpentine course is constantly altered by

winds, tides, and other phenomena. It may shift laterally as much
as ten miles in a single day. This kind of movement gains significance in places where the stream ordinarily lies sixty to seventy
miles offshore.

Hemingway was intrigued by what he called "the great blue
river," and there's little doubt this fascination was a paramount
element in his decision to make Key West his permanent address.
The sea provided a back door through which to escape from any
problems or pressures that troubled him. Too, he had developed
an insatiable appetite for saltwater fishing, and he was continu-
ally seeking greater challenges.

Eventually Hemingway would take thousands of big-game fish
from the Gulf Stream, but there would be other significant benefits from these experiences. The blue water would yield an enormous amount of material for works published during his lifetime,
as well as another, *Islands in the Stream*, that was not known to
the public until after his death.

◆　　◆　　◆

HEMINGWAY, PAULINE, AND BABY Patrick came back to Key West in
November 1928. He had fishing on his mind, but it would be awhile
before his next trip out on the water. Bumby, his son by Hadley, was
coming from France for the summer. Hemingway met him at the
dock in New York, but on their way back to Key West, he got the
news of his father's suicide. He sent Bumby on and detoured to
Chicago for the funeral and subsequent family arrangements.

When he returned just before Christmas, he was faced with
the difficult task of rewriting *A Farewell to Arms*. The novel was
on deadline, and in addition, Scribner's magazine had picked up
the serial rights. The task required five weeks of steady writing.
On January 22, 1929, it was finally completed and ready for
Perkins to pick up upon his arrival in Key West a week later.

Hemingway was free at last to fish with nothing else on his
mind. Since beginning work on the rewriting, he'd been able to

get away only a few times on Sundays. He wrote Perkins, telling him the Gulf Stream was "alive with fish" and that he'd caught an eight-foot-six-inch sailfish.

It took two months to get the novel into galley proofs, and during that time Hemingway devoted all of his time to fishing. He had again assembled the Mob—Strater, Pierce, and Dos Passos—and chartered Captain Bra's boat with Burge as mate. Being able to add Perkins to the crowd delighted Hemingway; he knew it would be excellent therapy for the serious and over-worked editor who had just begun the arduous task of digging through the trunk full of manuscripts brought to him by a new Scribner's writer, Thomas Wolfe.

The group again set up headquarters at the Fort Jefferson docks. As on the previous trip, both the weather and the fishing were excellent. Perkins had the time of his life, catching plenty of fish and thoroughly enjoying the variety of seafood dishes the crew consumed. Within a few days, his New York City pallor was replaced with a healthy tan.

Again, one particular event made the trip significant. The night before their departure, a Cuban commercial fishing boat pulled into the dock, and Hemingway, fluent in Spanish, began talking with the crew. The captain's knowledge of fishing impressed him, and in the evening of drinking and eating that followed, Hemingway paid special attention to all he said. Before they left, he had recorded Carlos Gutierrez's name and address. A chance encounter, but it would turn out that Gutierrez had by no means seen the last of Hemingway.

The next hiatus from Key West lasted for ten months, and the Hemingways returned in February 1930 to a different house that Lorine Thompson had rented for them. In the meantime, the publication of *A Farewell to Arms* had brought Hemingway national fame. Even more, he had sold the movie rights for twenty-four thousand dollars. For the first time since his marriage to Pauline, he felt he was financially independent.

The success of the novel ended the period of anonymity in his island haven and simultaneously marked the germination of the Hemingway legend. Members of the press were showing up for interviews, eager to accept and print virtually anything he told them. Because of his own journalistic experience, he knew what reporters wanted to hear, and he adorned his stories accordingly.

The annual gathering of the Mob took place in March, although this time its composition was somewhat different from before. Perkins, who had come to relish this annual event, was on hand, as was Strater. John Hermann, a Michigan native whom Hemingway had met in Europe, was wintering in Key West with his wife, and he agreed to join the gang. Burge Saunders was to be the one-man crew of the cabin cruiser rented for the trip to their usual destination—the Tortugas.

It was fortunate that they were well provisioned. The trip was intended to last a week, but a severe tropical storm kept them marooned for seventeen days. It was an adventure that no doubt caused great concern to those back at Key West, but the members of the Mob relished it. The food eventually ran out, but there was an abundance of fish and crawfish and conch. Perkins, whose catch of a fifty-eight-pound kingfish on the way out had already made the trip memorable, considered the experience of being stranded on the remote Caribbean island the adventure of his lifetime.

Hemingway had started work on a bullfighting book that had been on his mind for five years. It was going well until Dos Passos and his wife, Katy, arrived, at which time he temporarily abandoned the project for another trip to the Tortugas. Following that, the combination of a serious cut to his right index finger and a quick visit by MacLeish caused him further delay.

The schedule of activities in Hemingway's life made the period of January to June the best time to be in Key West. When May ended, he again went to New York to pick up Bumby for his summer visit, then proceeded on to Piggot to join Pauline.

Hemingway sometimes went to the Pilot House in the Key West channel to write. The structure was torched by vandals in the 1970s.

Bad luck stalked Hemingway during the latter half of 1930. He suffered a badly fractured arm in a car accident, and when he and Pauline came back to Key West at the beginning of 1931, he was still handicapped by the injury.

He managed to surround himself with plenty of company to soothe his miseries, though, including family and old and new friends. Despite his being partially disabled, Hemingway insisted on putting together the annual Tortugas trip. The Mob rented a sleek new charter boat for the expedition from Albert Pinder that was big enough for the seven people going out: veterans Hemingway, Perkins, Hermann, and Burge and newcomers Pat and Maude Morgan and Chub Weaver.

A number of problems plagued this outing, however. Max had to leave early, and soon after that a bad winter storm hit that kept the fishermen confined to the Fort Jefferson docks. With three

125

hundred pounds of fish on hand and ice running low, Hermann and Burge went back to Key West for a new supply. A combination of engine trouble and more bad weather delayed their return. By the time they returned, the fish had spoiled and Hemingway's mood had soured.

Yet there was one bright spot. Earlier in the trip they had run out of Bermuda onions, so Hemingway and Perkins, wanting to purchase some, approached a small Cuban fishing sloop that was tied up to the dock. The boat was extremely clean and orderly, and the captain, a deeply tanned and weathered native of the Canary Islands, made a lasting impression on Hemingway. His name was Gregorio Fuentes. Hemingway later remarked to Charles Thompson that if he ever should be able to have his own sport-fishing boat, Gregorio was the kind of man he wanted to put in charge of it. It was a wish that one day would come true.

◆　　◆　　◆

THE BROKEN ARM AND the jinxed fishing trip made the beginning of 1931 less than joyous, but there were events to come that would make it truly a milestone year.

Pauline had come to realize that Hemingway was determined to stay in Key West. It wasn't her first choice. She preferred Paris or the Mediterranean, but her husband's happiness was more important to her. In the early spring, Pauline and Lorine dedicated themselves to finding a suitable house. Generous Uncle Gus had said he'd purchase whatever place she chose.

What they finally decided upon was a two-story, Spanish-style mansion at 907 Whitehead Street. The house had been built in 1851 by a shipping tycoon, and it was constructed from coral stone that was quarried at the site. It was badly in need of renovation, but the Hemingways decided that most of the necessary work could be accomplished during their absence. They were going to Paris then on to Spain to follow the bullfights for additional research on the book in progress.

It didn't work out exactly as planned. When they came back in December, five weeks after Gregory was born, there was still much to be done. The upper part of the carriage house and servants' quarters, back of the main building, however, had been converted into a study. This provided Hemingway with a relatively calm atmosphere in which to work.

At the Hemingway Historical House, as it is now called, the "writing room" is what visitors are most interested in seeing, probably because it is a place they can readily identify with the legendary author. I once heard one of the tourists remark, "This is where the soul of Hemingway lives." If the observation is true, then Hemingway's is either a highly fragmented soul or an extremely mobile one, since the same thing has been said about many other places he lived or wrote about.

There is something missing that once more intimately associated the room with the main house: a narrow iron catwalk that connected it with the master bedroom. This feature was lost in a hurricane many years ago. Also, the lower level that Pauline converted into a cabana when the pool was built is now an office. The famous six-toed cats are still there, many generations removed from the first of these genetically flawed felines of which Hemingway was particularly fond. A couple dozen of them lounge around the premises. Sylvia Robards says they are so pampered and well fed that they are not inclined to disappear into the outside world.

"They don't wander off the property," Robards says, "so we don't even have a 'catnapping' problem."

At one time, with a constant deluge of kittens appearing, there was an adoption policy. Legal ramifications caused this to be abandoned, and today selective neutering keeps the population in check.

◆　◆　◆

ONCE INSTALLED IN HIS writing room away from the bustle of activity in the house, Hemingway devoted all his time to revising

Hemingway's writing room was on the second floor of a small building behind the main house in Key West.

the bulky, 150,000-word manuscript of his bullfighting book. He completed it in mid-January, but instead of going fishing, he began working on several short stories. The "juices" were flowing, and he wanted to keep working. This period of intense activity resulted in a number of the short stories that appeared in a 1933 Scribner's collection, *Winner Take Nothing*.

He abandoned the writing temporarily in February to make a quick trip with Captain Bra and Charles Thompson. They hit a school of big kingfish between the Marquesas and Tortugas that later sold for enough to nearly pay for the trip, and Hemingway's catch of a five-and-a-half-foot barracuda helped him forget the hard-driving schedule he had been following.

A spell of bad weather interrupted their idyll and forced them to return to Key West. Once it had passed, they went back to Fort Jefferson to resume the fishing. Hemingway was aware that there were giant billfish in the Gulf Stream, and he dreamed of doing battle with them. There were two problems. First, sport fishermen didn't know much about fishing for them: marlin and swordfish were almost exclusively the quarry of commercial fishermen. Second, the tackle available at that time wasn't adequate to handle heavy fish that could make long, line-burning runs.

Sailfish and tarpon were the "big fish" of the time. Both produced specimens well over a hundred pounds and were enormously challenging to fishermen who had somewhat rudimentary gear. Species such as kingfish, dolphin, amberjack, and barracuda could also be tough to handle and provided plenty of action.

A number of smaller fish—yellowtails, groupers, snappers, and muttonfish—were prime food fare on the long trips. Yet big catches of any kind (or kinds) of fish were brought in and sold at the dock, helping offset the cost of fuel and other expenses.

Emilio Burgohy, a Conch who has lived all his life less than a block from the Hemingway House, told me that he has a special memory of that particular period.

"I was just a little boy at the time, but in the afternoons when Mr. Hemingway's boat came in, we'd run down to the dock. He almost always had caught something, but before he did anything with them, he'd give each of us kids one fish apiece to take home.

"I'll never forget this kindness. Those were hard times. The Depression was on and everybody was suffering, especially the poor folks. Me and my family had Mr. Hemingway to thank for a lot of meals!"

Today, Emilio is retired, but he's reminded daily of the past. His wife, Viola, is a member of the Hemingway House staff, and occasionally he does various odd jobs around the premises.

13

THE PILAR

THE FIRST PERSON TO gain prominence in big-game fishing was Zane Grey, the famous author of early western adventure novels. Grey traveled all over the world in his three-masted schooner searching for new fishing adventures. He was a major authority on a variety of species and the techniques with which to catch them, and he wrote a book on big-game fishing that Hemingway read in 1928. In a typical reaction, Hemingway made a vow that he would match or surpass Grey's level of expertise.

Ironically, some years later when Hemingway himself was high-profile in the sport, he turned down an invitation from Grey to participate in a two-man worldwide fishing expedition. For some inexplicable reason, Hemingway believed that Grey wanted to trade off his reputation. It was a totally illogical assumption because even then, as now, Grey was considered to be one of the greatest big-game fishermen who ever lived.

The publication of *Death in the Afternoon* did little to enhance Hemingway's literary reputation. Few critics gave it good marks, and sales were disappointing. The project was personally gratifying, though. He had written what he considered to be an authoritative text on the subject. That judgment was correct. It became a cult book, and today, sixty years after it first appeared, it continues to enjoy that reputation.

He wasn't in Key West when *Death in the Afternoon* was released, but the bad reviews seemed only to increase his energy. Once back in the writing room at Whitehead Street he quickly completed three stories for *Scribner's* magazine, one of which—"A Clean, Well-Lighted Place"—is among his best known. It was another of his short works that eventually became a movie.

◆　　◆　　◆

IF ANY SINGLE EVENT could be considered as marking the emergence of the "Papa" myth in Key West, it would have to be the delivery of the *Pilar* in May 1934. This signaled the beginning of a special association between man and machine that would be immortalized in both fact and fiction.

The *Pilar* was the thirty-eight-foot fishing boat Hemingway had ordered from a New York shipyard when he and Pauline returned from an African safari. He used a three-thousand-dollar advance from *Esquire* magazine for future articles as a down payment on the total cost of seventy-five hundred dollars, confident he could pay off the remainder relatively quickly.

It was the right time for this important acquisition. Hemingway was now a successful author, and his fame and wealth were increasing. Having his own boat gave him a new sense of freedom and felicity and enhanced his personality. He could go fishing whenever he pleased, leaving any land-spawned annoyances or interruptions far behind.

At first, Hemingway and his fishing companions manned the boat, but he was already thinking of assembling a full-time crew. His own crew would obviate his having to fool with prearrangements for trips and also give him the option of staying at sea for however long he wished, with capable hands on board.

By this time Hemingway had become a competent seaman and a skilled fisherman, much admired by his contemporaries for his strength and stamina. He had the ability to boat big fish quickly, combining his impressive physical strength and some special fighting techniques he devised. This was a skill he eventually developed to the point of being regarded as an authority on the subject.

In 1930 Uncle Gus had offered to finance an African safari for Hemingway and Pauline, and in the fall of 1933 the plan went into motion. The couple first traveled to Spain then on to Paris, where they were joined by Charles Thompson. The party of three reached Mombasa on December 8 and were met by Philip Percival, one of the most respected professional hunters in Kenya. They hunted in the bush for two months then returned to Mombasa for a short rest.

The dream of having his own boat had been with Hemingway for a long time, and it's likely that an experience following the African hunt may have hastened his decision to make it come true. Hemingway thought it would be fun to take Percival deep-sea fishing in the Indian Ocean. He had observed that it somewhat resembled the Caribbean, and he felt it was bound to have fishing potential. The excursion included Thompson and young Alfred Vanderbilt, who wanted to come along and offered to pay half the expenses.

What no one could foresee was that the chartered boat, the *Xanadu*, was a wornout tub that lacked any of the essentials or equipment necessary for such a venture. The engine was faulty, and about twenty minutes' running time was the best the Hindu engineer aboard could manage. The group's good spirits and enthusiasm turned what could have been a miserable experience into an adventure. They nailed a plank across the stern and manufactured rudimentary fighting chairs. With Hemingway and Thompson maneuvering the boat, Percival and Vanderbilt managed to catch an impressive mixed bag of fish, including dolphins and sailfish. Hemingway immediately filed away the Indian Ocean as another area he wanted to revisit in the future.

Hemingway and Pauline spent a couple of weeks in Paris before returning home. In April when the *Ile de France* docked in New York, he hurried to the shipbuilder to order his boat. He had specific design ideas, and he wanted it to be a strictly functional craft. He recalled the details in a magazine article he wrote for *Holiday* in 1949:

> *Pilar* was built to be a fishing machine that would be a good sea boat in the heaviest kind of weather, have a minimum cruising range of five hundred miles, and sleep seven people. She carries three hundred gallons of gasoline in her tanks and one hundred and fifty gallons of water. On a long trip she can carry another hundred gallons of gas in small drums in her forward cockpit and the same extra amount of water in demijohns. She carries, when loaded full, 2400 pounds of ice.
>
> Wheeler Shipyard, of New York, built her hull and modified it to our specifications, and we have made various changes in her since. She is a really sturdy boat, sweet in any kind of sea, and she has a very low-cut stem with a large wooden roller to bring big fish over. The flying bridge is so sturdy and so reinforced below you can fight fish from the top of the house.

There was special significance in the boat's name. *Pilar* is the patron saint of the Catholic bullfight shrine in Zaragoza, Spain, but it was also a pet name Hemingway gave Pauline early in their relationship. Later, he would use it again for a prominent character in *For Whom the Bell Tolls*.

The timing of the *Pilar*'s arrival could not have been better. A number of Hemingway's friends were visiting: John and Katy Dos Passos; Gerald and Sara Murphy, whom he had met in Paris; and Ada MacLeish. Hemingway's younger brother, Leicester ("Les"), and Al Dudeck, a pal from Petosky, Michigan, arrived after crossing the Gulf of Mexico on a small sailboat Les had built.

These people, along with the local "regulars," participated in a series of short trips Hemingway made in order to familiarize himself with the *Pilar*. While his guests fished or when the boat was just cruising, he stayed busy checking every functional and operational detail. The boat was to be his counterpart, so to speak, and he wanted to know its every mood and idiosyncrasy.

There was a problem of divided priorities, however. The African experience affected him profoundly, and immediately upon his return, he began work on a novel that he said would be "an absolutely true account of a month's hunting in Africa." He also wished to use the book to reveal many of the sensuous feelings and memories the safari had evoked.

He developed several lists to be used as guidelines in the composition of the book, none of which was included in the finished product. One of the lists gives an idea, though, of what he wanted to encompass:

> To stay in places and to leave, to trust, to distrust, to no longer believe and believe again, to care about fishes, the different winds, the changes of the seasons, to see what happens, to be out in boats, to sit in a saddle, to watch the snow come, to watch it go, to hear rain on a tent, to know where I can find what I want.

Initially, the book was entitled *The Highlands of Africa*, but later the title was changed to *Green Hills of Africa*.

Hemingway managed to accommodate his two dominant urges on about a fifty-fifty basis. Normally, when he had a work in progress, it was his principal mistress, but the *Pilar* put things in a different light. His exhilaration at having this sleek new possession was still a powerful force that would not be diminished until he could devote his full attention to her. But he could not pay proper homage to the boat until the writing task was completed.

The first fishing triumph aboard the *Pilar* resulted in mixed emotions and had a somewhat clouded aftermath. He reported what happened in a May 25, 1934, letter to Arnold Gingrich:

> And incidentally we caught, day before yest, what I hope is the Atlantic record for sailfish—going out at 2:30 from here after a big morning's work. Weighed 119½ lbs. 9 feet and ¾ inch long. 35 inches girth. . . . The hell of it is he was hooked by a Jesuit priest who doesn't want his name in the papers as he was supposed to be doing something else here beside fish. He had just fought and lost a sailfish taken by a shark after 14 jumps. He had just put out and hooked this one. His left arm has arthritis and was in bad shape from the first fish so he turned this one over to me after one jump. I had him 44 minutes. I couldn't believe any sailfish could pull and so I thought he must be foul hooked. He was so beautifully proportioned he didn't show his weight,
>
> I won't claim him because I didn't hook him so am trying to get Father McGrath to claim him. Anyway will enter him for the Atlantic record as a fish. That is a sailfish, Bo. . . . Seventy five is a hell of a fine one and I've never heard of one that was a hundred. This baby was 119½ on tested scales before eight witnesses four hours after he was caught.

When Father McGrath returned to Miami, he wrote an anonymous story for the *Herald*, accompanied by a picture of Hemingway and the fish. In the article, the priest claimed that Hemingway caught the fish. The upshot was that Hemingway went along with the story, and the mounted specimen was hung in the Miami Rod and Reel Club acknowledging "his" catch as the Atlantic record. He later told his friend Charles Thompson that the inaccuracy did not bother him. "It's their lie, not mine," he said.

◆　　◆　　◆

ALTHOUGH THE "PAPA" PART of the Hemingway legend was nurtured into full bloom in Key West, it didn't have its origin there. He began using the self-proclaimed nickname during the Paris years while he was still in his twenties. Its first appearance in Key West was probably in a letter dictated and sent to Charles Thompson after Hemingway's car wreck in Montana in 1929 in which he broke his right arm. He signed it with his left hand: "Poor Old Papa."

Following the publication of *Green Hills of Africa*, in which Pauline was referred to as P.O.M. (Poor Old Mama), she had a footstool made for Hemingway with the letters P.O.P. (Poor Old Papa) on it.

Key West old-timers said that the sobriquet really came into common usage after his return from the Spanish Civil War in 1937, no doubt with his encouragement.

He was still under forty, but this time it stuck.

◆   ◆   ◆

WORK ON THE AFRICAN book kept Hemingway in Key West during the summer of 1934, and although he may have yearned for the western mountains and trout fishing, the presence of the *Pilar* made staying at home much more bearable. A longer trip into the Gulf Stream was not yet possible, but he was laying plans for one by late July.

A major effort toward assembling a crew was underway. Hemingway had begun corresponding with Carlos Gutierrez, the Cuban fishing-boat captain he had met in 1929 in the Dry Tortugas. Gutierrez had served aboard Josie Russell's boat, the *Anita*, the year before, and Hemingway felt he was the best choice for the job. In early July, Gutierrez accepted.

In the meantime, Arnold Samuelson, a would-be writer from Minnesota, had shown up at Hemingway's door, and even though he had no experience or qualifications, he was signed on as another crew member. Samuelson was hired because he absolutely idolized Hemingway.

The impact of this mistake was soon felt. Hemingway had wanted Josie Russell to be at the wheel of the *Pilar* on its first major Gulf Stream cruise, but Russell had to decline. That left him with Gutierrez as the only proficient mate.

Hemingway fished for more than fifty days, but by early September he had neglected the African book too long. He came back to Key West and wrote diligently until midmonth then went back to sea again. When he returned near the end of October, it was time for the final spurt. Despite minor interruptions as some members of the Mob arrived, *Green Hills of Africa* was completed in first draft on November 16.

In January 1935, after a Christmas visit to Piggot with Pauline and the boys, and with no immediate work on the book pending, he could enjoy a relaxed routine of fishing and drinking with his local and visiting friends. He planned to go after tuna in the late spring, so the short trips out with the *Pilar* to his favorite spots in the various channels and Gulf Stream helped him get into shape. It was a three-month idyll, and it was the last of these he would experience in Key West. Events of the near future, some pleasant and others not, would alter his halcyon island existence enormously.

On the happy side, the *Pilar*'s long-range capabilities increased Hemingway's desire to seek out more distant fishing areas. Most of his summer was spent far from Key West. He tackled some new big-game species and made acquaintances who were to influence his life for many years to come.

On the other hand, natural disaster played a part in the changing scenario. Soon after his return a monster hurricane hit the Keys, and while Key West was spared most of its fury and Hemingway's beloved *Pilar* rode out the storm, Lower and Upper Matacombe Keys were virtually wiped out. Hundreds were killed, and the Florida East Coast Railroad was permanently put out of business.

This catastrophe also marked the beginning of the end of the isolation that the Conchs and artists like Hemingway, Dos Passos,

Strater, and others cherished. The state and federal governments decided to save the Keys, and within three years a new overseas highway permitted automobile travel all the way to Key West.

However, the real coup de grâce to Hemingway's tranquil island life was delivered when Martha Gelhorn, "the beautiful blonde in the black dress," approached Hemingway in Sloppy Joe's bar in December 1936. Her appearance began a liaison that sent his domestic life into a tailspin from which it never recovered.

PART 4

The Caribbean

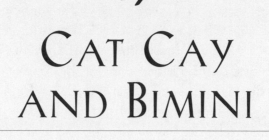

14

CAT CAY
AND BIMINI

ALONG THE BEACH AT Cat Cay at night, the palm trees are sil-houetted against the sky like black tarantulas, and the combers whisper softly as they sweep up onto the sandy beach. The tranquility is hypnotic, and it's easy to get lost in time. This is the kind of atmosphere that Hemingway found so desirable when he first visited Cat Cay and Bimini in 1935.

Bimini is just a few miles to the north, but unlike Cat Cay it is no longer a peaceful, low-key haven. Great changes have taken place over the years. Today Bimini is overdeveloped and bustling with people, both residents and tourists. Meanwhile, Cat Cay has retained its idyllic, pristine qualities only because it is a private island protected against intrusion.

Hemingway wrote about Bimini and made it famous, but he also spent much time at Cat Cay fishing, writing, and relaxing with Pauline and the boys. Some of the wealthy big-game fishermen who were his friends had homes on the island. There were also excellent dining facilities and, for a couple of years, a casino.

Today the island is operated by a corporation based in Miami and remains the exclusive domain of members and guests.

There are a few exceptions. One is for participants in the Forty-fifth Annual Cat Cay Yacht Club's Invitational Tuna Tournament along with their crew and guests. In fact, I'm on the island as the guest of John Morris, one of the competitors, and for the past four days we've been back and forth on Tuna Fish Alley, the legendary stretch of water off Cat and Gun Cays that was once considered to be the top bluefin tuna spot in the world. John has brought both of his sport-fishing boats over, a sixty-foot Jim Smith and a forty-five-foot Rybovich. John is fishing from the Smith and his best friend, Kevin Walkup, from the other.

There have been tuna tournaments at Cat Cay since the 1930s, but this particular one began in 1944. At that time, the number of tuna that showed up on their spring migration was phenomenal. For an individual boat to land six to a dozen fish in the course of the tournament was not unusual.

That isn't true anymore. This year, for instance, as the end of the tournament approaches, not a single tuna has been entered. A few small schools have been spotted, but none have produced any action. Each day the drama increases, and even though I'm only an observer, I'm well aware of the tension John and Kevin and the rest of the participants are feeling.

In 1988 John won the tournament with a 743-pounder he caught in the final forty-five minutes of the last day. He's hoping fervently that Lady Luck will pay him another eleventh-hour visit. John may be no more avid a Hemingway fan and admirer than millions of others around the world, but he's able to express it in a more prominent manner. John owns Bass Pro Shops, one of the nation's largest sporting-goods retail and mail-order catalog companies. The centerpiece of the company's huge store in Springfield, Missouri, is Hemingway's, a restaurant decorated with items from John's collection of authentic memorabilia. Earlier in the week I asked John how his intense interest in Hemingway came about.

Today Cat Cay is rimmed with private residences, but the area was mostly deserted when Hemingway discovered it for himself.

"It goes way back," he said, "starting with *The Old Man and the Sea*. I remember reading the book when I was very young and also my father taking me to see the movie that starred Spencer Tracy when I was still at an impressionable young age. I don't think there's a fisherman anywhere, regardless of age, who couldn't be deeply touched and excited by it.

"Growing up in Missouri, I was about as far away from the ocean as you can get, but I spun great daydreams about the ocean and the stupefying big fish. Later on I was inspired by seeing Hemingway's house in Key West and by reading *To Have and Have Not*, where he talked about the early days when the fishing was really good.

"Then, about fourteen years ago Alex Adler, a young red-headed charter captain in Islamorada, Florida, called and asked if I wanted to sign up for some big-game fishing for giant bluefin

Aboard his custom sport-fishing boat, John Morris and I fished much as Hemingway did in the famed Tuna Fish Alley.

tuna. I'd never heard of them until he called me. I was in my late twenties and just getting started in business, so chartering his boat was something that took a big bite out of my pocketbook. But it was something I really wanted to do, so I signed up for three days of fishing.

"The first day out with Alex, I encountered a bluefin larger than any I've ever hooked since. To this day I don't know exactly how big it was, because after fighting it for more than two hours we broke it off at the wire before it could be landed. I vividly recall Alex and the mate telling me that they had boated an eight-hundred-pound tuna without any difficulty, and they firmly believed that this fish had to be well over a thousand pounds.

"Anyway, this experience permanently fired up my enthusiasm and love for the giant bluefin. From the strike to the run to the end of the long fight, there is no fish anywhere to compare with it. The bluefin is one of the most powerful and magnificent creatures in the ocean.

146

"I've been fishing with Alex every year since, spending my main vacation to go back to Bimini and Cat Cay. I began participating in the Cat Cay tournament in 1988, and I won it. No matter what happens this time, I'm ahead of the game. All things considered, I guess I always will be."

The follow-up to this story is that John has not won since that first time, but his friend Kevin won the 1991 tournament with a 740-pound fish.

Participating in tournaments isn't the extent of John's interest in the sport, by the way.

"There's a declining population of giant bluefins due to increased commercial fishing by the Japanese and other factors. As a result, I've devoted a lot of time in recent years to fisheries conservation, trying to help find a way to save this great resource. I guess it could be called my way of paying Hemingway back for introducing me to the thrill of big-game fishing."

◆　　◆　　◆

BIMINI HAD BEEN BECKONING to Hemingway since he first heard of this Bahamian island paradise. Friends told him about its unspoiled beauty and relaxed atmosphere, and he had read in Zane Grey's account that sixteen of twenty-nine world records were taken there. Since Bimini is 232 nautical miles northeast of Key West, however, Hemingway knew that until he had his own boat, such a venture would not be possible. It's quite likely that thoughts of this particular destination played a major role in the decision to buy his own boat.

The delivery of the *Pilar* opened the door to this opportunity. Once it had been proven seaworthy on short runs out of Key West and to Cuba, he was ready to take it on an extended cruise. The lure of Bimini's beauty and thoughts of world-record fish made it his choice as a destination.

The first attempt—with Mike Strater, John and Katy Dos Passos, and crew members Bread Pinder and Hamilton Adams aboard—was aborted after Hemingway accidentally shot himself in the legs while firing at a shark with a .22 pistol. The group returned to Key West so Hemingway could be treated. He was not badly injured physically, but he felt humiliated by the event.

The next try, a week later, came off without incident, the only difference being that Charles Thompson went along in place of Mike Strater. Everyone found the quaint and somewhat primitive environment exciting and delightfully tranquil. The island enjoyed virtual isolation except for a few private yachts that paid occasional visits and a Pan American seaplane that made scheduled flights from the mainland.

The tuna were late in showing up, and Hemingway's first experience with them came in May. Charlie Cook, the manager at Cat Cay, hooked a big one in the morning and fought it until afternoon. Hemingway arrived on the *Pilar,* took over from the exhausted Cook, and battled the tuna until dark. When it was finally brought alongside, the person with the gaff missed, and the tuna made another strong run. Before Hemingway could bring the fish in, the sharks arrived. By the time it was hauled into the boat, all that remained were the backbone, tail, and head.

The marathon contest had attracted a number of spectator boats, but a rainstorm drove all but one of them back to shore. The single remaining craft was a yacht owned by an international sportsman, William B. Leeds, who took the drenched Hemingway party aboard his craft to dry out and spend the night. Leeds owned a Thompson submachine gun, and with Hemingway's anger at the shark attack still at a boiling point, the weapon immediately caught his attention. The next morning it was in his possession, though the details of the transaction never became known.

Hemingway's use of the Tommy gun created some controversy, since gunning sharks that were attacking hooked tuna or marlin simply spilled more blood. This drawback was illustrated when Mike Strater was fighting a monster marlin that observers said would have topped a thousand pounds. When the sharks moved in, Hemingway sprayed them with bullets, turning the water pink and increasing the pack's feeding frenzy. An hour later when the fish was boated, what remained weighed five hundred pounds. The Thompson sub, however, provided the opportunity for many other theatrics, and it remained a standard fixture on the *Pilar*. It was also immortalized in the shark attack sequence that appears in *Islands in the Stream*. The major triumph of the Bimini excursion came when Hemingway landed the first unmutilated tuna ever recorded. It was a feat that demonstrated what a combination of skill and great strength could accomplish. Within days, he did it again, and the feat quickly became a sort of Hemingway trademark.

Another incident illustrates Hemingway's prowess with big fish. In early June he hooked a giant mako shark and landed it in thirty minutes. It weighed 785 pounds, only 12 pounds short of a

Cat Cay has always been a private island, and it still offers the same privacy and tranquility that Hemingway enjoyed here when he first visited in 1935.

149

world record. That proved to be heady stuff for him. In a letter to Max Perkins he boasted that he had personally changed the whole system of big-game fishing around Bimini. He also claimed to have taught Tommy Shevlin, a wealthy young sportsman from Miami, the techniques that allowed him to boat his 636-pound Atlantic-record marlin.

Hemingway's letter of June 4, 1935, to Perkins illustrates this new ego boost:

> We had a marlin at least a third bigger than Mike's [Mike Strater's] whipped and at the boat when the hook pulled out. After the goddamndest fight you ever saw. He made 22 jumps clean out of water and when he had out nearly half mile of line looked like the damned Normandie. I had him at the boat in 28 minutes. He jumped himself to death just as Mike's fish did. But the hook pulled out. Would have beaten the world's record by plenty. Well what the hell. They are there. But you come down when you get this letter and we will put the heat to them. Plenty small ones too but we are using 8 and ten pound tuna trolling. Caught the two tuna in one hour ten and in 48 minutes. All the boats there had been fishing four years and nobody caught any. Have won 350 bucks betting we would with the rich boys. Plenty rich boys. But now no bets.

Hemingway's discovery of Bimini provided him another idyllic place that he could urge his friends and associates in the literary community to visit. He asserted that the island was one of the finest places he had ever been. One expression of his enthusiasm appears in a letter to Sara Murphy in July 1935:

> You would love this place Sara. It's in the middle of the Gulf Stream and every breeze is a cool one. The water is so clear you think you will strike bottom when you have 10 fathoms under your keel. There is every kind of fish, altho the big marlin and tuna seem to have passed. There is a pretty good hotel (The

Compleat Angler: Mrs. Helen Duncombe) and we have a room there now because there have been rain squalls at night lately and so I cant sleep on the roof of the boat. That's not a very nautical term but a fine cool place to sleep.

He went on to add:

We bring our drinking water and ice and fresh vegetables on the pilot boat that comes once a week from Miami. There is no kind of sickness on the island and the average age of people in the cemetery is 85. About ⅔ of population is black. It is under the British flag and there is only one policeman who was gone to Nassau for 2 weeks. We have celebrations on the Queen's Birthday, the Jubilee, The Prince of Wales Birthday, the 4th of July, and will celebrate the 14th of July, getting drunk on all of these.

The summer idyll ended in August. When Hemingway returned to Bimini the following June, a number of the wealthiest sport fishermen in the world—Michael Lerner, Tommy Shevlin, Winston Guest, Tommy Gifford, Kip Farrington, Colonel Richard Cooper, and many others—were present at the island. Hemingway's growing fame as an author, and his angling prowess, gained him their respect and admiration, and he was soon fishing and socializing with them.

Hemingway was by this time the most famous person in Key West, and it was not long until he held that honor in Bimini as well. His renown spread throughout the black population, too, mainly because of his boxing skills. Hemingway's practice of using this sport as a means of challenge and intimidation dated back to his early days in Paris. At Bimini he issued a standing offer of $250 to any black who could stay in the ring with him for three three-minute rounds. No one ever collected. He also gained additional fame by knocking out a wealthy publisher who was visiting the island. The delighted natives celebrated the event by writing a Calypso song about the "big slob" from Key West.

Hemingway's new acquaintances added a considerable degree of luxury to his life, including access to Cat Cay, which then belonged to New York advertising executive Lou Wasey. Pauline and the boys often stayed there. Still, he had reservations about his association with the rich, sensing that it might somehow harm his integrity as a writer. He told Arnold Gingrich, editor of *Esquire*, that he and Pauline were only peasants among the rich and famous at Bimini.

Hemingway had expressed an awareness of this danger in "The Snows of Kilimanjaro," when Harry Morgan, the writer dying of gangrene, blames his rich wife for his failure, but also himself:

> But, in yourself, you said that you would write about these people; about the very rich; that you were really not of them but a spy in their country; that you would leave it and write of it and for once it would be written by someone who knew what he was writing of. But he would never do it, because each day of not writing, of comfort, of being that which he despised, dulled his ability and softened his will to work so that, finally, he did no work at all.

Marjorie Kinnan Rawlings, author of *The Yearling*, visited Bimini and became a friend of Hemingway. She was another of the writers in Max Perkins's stable that also included F. Scott Fitzgerald and William Faulkner, and she was able to see the reasons for his apprehension. Rawlings found the wealthy sporting people delightful companions but worlds away from her in most ways. In her opinion, they enjoyed life immensely without being sensitive to it.

Hemingway remained at Bimini for only about a month and a half in 1936, spending as much time writing and discussing upcoming projects with editors as he spent fishing. He did manage to take one trophy tuna, a 514-pound fish he hooked off Gun Cay that required seven hours to bring to the gaff. The brief interlude at Bimini that summer was simply a period of calm before further storms.

15

A Reminiscence

THE NEXT HIATUS FROM Bimini, which lasted from mid-July 1936 until late May 1937, was one of the most tumultuous periods of Hemingway's career. Martha Gelhorn came into his life, portending a split with Pauline. He became intensely involved in the Spanish Civil War and spent forty-five days in Spain, where he covered the conflict for the North American Newspaper Alliance. His return to Bimini is vividly recalled by someone who was present on the scene.

"I first fished with Hemingway in April of 1937 when he came back from the Spanish Civil War," Roy Bosche tells me. "He called me up and said he wanted to go to Bimini to relax and work on a book. Mike Lerner had offered the loan of his house, and Hemingway wanted to bring Pauline, Greg, and Patrick with him. He asked me to meet with him to discuss the matter.

"The plan was suitable to me. I'd known Hemingway since 1935, and I was at Bimini when he landed the first unmutilated tuna ever taken by a sport fisherman. I looked forward to working for him. We met at a restaurant in Miami to discuss the details, then went back to Key West to get the boat."

We're sitting on Roy's screened-in back porch in Lake Park, Florida, enjoying the fresh, cool air in the wake of a February downpour. At seventy-eight years of age, he could pass for sixty, and it's obvious that his love of fishing has not diminished in the ten years since he retired. His memory hasn't either. It's still razor sharp, even regarding small incidents and exact dates.

"It was one of the most enjoyable summers of my life," he continues. "Ernest wrote in the mornings and we fished in the afternoons. Caught a few marlin and plenty of good eating fish. Pauline and the kids often accompanied us. She was a fine lady, and I got to be pals with Greg and Pat. Also, I found Hemingway to be a great guy. He was fun to fish with and was always open to suggestions and new ideas. One thing, though, when you were aboard the *Pilar*, it was clear that there was only one captain—Hemingway.

"His fishing routine was different during this period because there were a lot of interruptions. He was back and forth to Washington and New York a couple of times. Also, the war in Spain was on his mind. He went back over a couple of months later. It was also different in that he hadn't assembled his usual Cuban crew. I guess it was because he was pretty sure this trip would be brief.

"In midsummer, Mike and his wife came down and needed the house, so Hemingway took Lou Wasey, owner of Cat Cay, up on an offer to use the Strong House on that nearby island. We fished out of there until August. Lou, incidentally, had a big advertising agency in New York, and he used Cat Cay as a place to entertain his clients. Barbasol was his biggest account at the time.

"Of course, big fish—tuna and marlin—were Hemingway's favorite quarry, and in those days tackling them was a real challenge. Both the tackle and the fishing boats were primitive by

The small lighthouse marker that Hemingway and his pals used for target practice is still in the harbor at Cat Cay.

today's standards. What gave Hemingway the edge in these contests was that he was strong as a bull, and this, along with his skill in handling big fish, made it possible for him to put fish in the boat fast.

"One major problem was that there were no drag systems on the old reels, which meant a big, heavy fish couldn't be slowed or stopped. As a result, everything was mutilated by sharks before it could be landed.

"Mike Lerner and Tommy Gifford deserve credit for a dramatic change in that situation. They had ideas for a new type of custom big-game reel. They met with Fred Cretin, who had a little machine shop called Fin Nor. He was a German machinist whom Tommy knew well. Fred said he knew nothing about fishing, but if they'd put on paper what they wanted, he could build it.

"Frankly, the first ones ever produced are as good as any later ones, and it should be mentioned that this wasn't the only advancement in tackle that Lerner and Shevlin were responsible for. They deserve a lot of credit for many of the improvements. Not only that, but Lerner was the main force behind the creation of the International Game Fish Association. Hemingway later made many major contributions to the organization.

"Something else. Flying bridges weren't standard. Hemingway realized that topside controls would be an advantage, so he installed them on the *Pilar*, using an automobile steering wheel. That was considered pretty innovative."

Roy has reasons for being less than impressed by today's tackle, electronic gear, and fishing craft.

"These things have taken a lot of the fun out of it because there's nothing left to do anymore. It's all high-tech, and all of the obstacles we used to face have been overcome. In the old days we were always trying to improve. For example, we didn't have much choice in fishing line. Cortland's 39-thread Green Stripe was what most fishermen used and thought was the best. We'd sit around at night trying to figure out knots that wouldn't allow the line to cut itself. We'd experiment, pulling on each other's lines to see how well the knots worked, and sometimes betting on them.

"Hemingway used the heaviest and toughest stuff he could find. He had a 15-O Hardy reel loaded with 54-thread line and a custom split-bamboo rod. With no drag on the reel, he fashioned a piece of *lignum vitae* wood that he could apply to the spool to slow it down. It worked, but sometimes on a long run, the wood would be literally smoking!

"One of the things I remember most fondly are the wonderful people who came to Bimini and Cat Cay in those days: the Shevlins, Lerners, Giffords, Masons, Winston Guest, Kip Farrington, and many others. They were, without exception, gracious, unpretentious, and friendly folks. People who love the sea and fishing seem to be more relaxed."

Gun Cay is adjacent to Cat Cay, and Tuna Fish Alley runs nearby.

The Bimini of today is vastly different from the island Roy first fished out of in the early 1930s.

"First of all, at the peak fishing times, there might be as many as ten boats at the dock. Some people stayed aboard, and others stayed at The Compleat Angler, a small rooming house and restaurant built by Mrs. Helen Duncombe, whose late husband had been commissioner of the island during the 1920s. It had the only accommodations on the island, and it was the main gathering place in the evenings. One night after Hemingway finished the book he was working on, *To Have and Have Not*, he read parts of it to the crowd at Mrs. Duncombe's.

Nowadays, The Compleat Angler is the main tourist attraction on the island, with the walls plastered with pictures of Hemingway and quotes from his books. That's because for a while after he discovered Bimini, he sometimes rented a room from Mrs. Duncombe as a getaway spot where he could do some writing.

Later, when several of his fishing pals built homes on Cat Cay, he always had a place to stay there. It was a choice that guaranteed more privacy. Pauline and the boys liked it better, too.

"When I think of Cat Cay, one humorous episode always comes to mind. It happened when Philip Percival, the famous African hunter who guided Hemingway's safari, came as a guest. He'd recently been knighted, and he brought with him a big-bore double rifle obtained in England. I don't know what caliber it was, but the cartridges looked as big as a broomstick!

"Hemingway, Tommy Shevlin, and Charlie Cook, manager of the island, were down at the dock looking at the rifle. About that time, Mike Lerner and Tommy Gifford pulled in to gas up the boat. The rifle was loaded, and as Mike and Tommy walked up, Hemingway snapped it to his shoulder and took a shot at a bird flying over.

"Mike asked him what it was, and Hemingway said it was a shotgun. He told Mike to take a shot at a hawk that had just appeared. Well, the recoil nearly broke Mike's shoulder, but after a few drinks, everybody got a lot braver. That's when the fun began.

"There's a little lighthouse on the breakwater at the entrance to the harbor at Cat Cay, and these guys decided to try to shoot the top off it with that elephant gun. They took turns, and the big bullets started taking their toll. In the meantime, Lou Wasey walked up, and he stood there calmly smoking his pipe as the shooting continued. I was standing beside him and asked why he didn't stop them. I'll never forget his answer.

"'Roy,' he said, 'I'm not worried. There are five of them shooting, and I'm going to get paid five times for that lighthouse.'

"Knowing Lou, I'm sure he did."

Roy remembered another amusing incident that had to do with Hemingway's relish for boxing.

"Tom Heeney was a heavyweight boxer who had once faced Gene Tunney, and Hemingway arranged to have what he called an 'exhibition' bout with the old pro. It was known that in these 'friendly' matches where the opponents were supposed to take it easy, Hemingway would sometimes sneak in a real Sunday punch. Someone alerted Heeney to this ploy, and when it happened, he was ready. Heeney simply leaned back and made Hemingway miss, then dropped him with a sharp left hook.

"It taught Hemingway a lesson, but he held no grudge. Heeney became a good friend, and Hemingway often boasted of having sparred with him."

Roy got a distant look in his eyes when he told me of the old days on Tuna Fish Alley. As he spoke, I could understand why.

"As far as the fishing is concerned, all I can say is that we had no trouble catching them. There were so damn many tuna that you couldn't miss! We used to get heavy southwest winds that pushed the Stream into the lee shores of Cat Cay and Gun Cay. When you came out of the cut between the islands, you didn't have to hunt for them: they were there. They didn't name it Tuna Fish Alley for nothing!

"All you had to do was head north and begin trolling. Hooking up with fish was virtually certain, but we had one problem. There's a sharp dropoff that parallels the islands, and because our boats were pretty slow, the tuna too often could make it to the edge and cut the line. We couldn't stop 'em and we couldn't catch up with 'em.

"We also didn't have the advantage of tuna towers. They didn't come along until after World War II. The first I recall seeing was one built by Johnny Rybovich, the famous boat designer. Our method was blind trolling, but as I indicated, it was good enough.

"I don't doubt that there are fewer giant bluefins caught today than in the past, and I'm sure commercial fishing is the main culprit. However, the weather cycle is a factor that's been overlooked as part of the cause. The kind of southwest winds we used to have seasonally aren't dependable anymore, and they're necessary for success."

Roy last saw Hemingway in 1955 in Havana, and as he sat and talked with him on the *Pilar*, he saw something that was especially meaningful.

"I noticed that the fighting chair I made for him back in the Cat Cay days was still in place on the boat. That was a nice memorial, and a reminder of some very good times!"

HAVANA

FROM MY ROOM IN the Riviera Hotel I can look out over Havana's harbor toward Morro Castle, the centuries-old fortress that guards the harbor entrance. It is a view similar to the one Hemingway described in "Marlin off the Morro: A Cuban Letter," an article he wrote for *Esquire* magazine in 1933.

The window pane, however, is heavily coated with grime, considerably diminishing the clarity of the vista. It is 1978, nearly twenty years since Castro seized power, and I'd be willing to wager that it hasn't been washed since. The battered and thread-bare furniture in the room seems to be a victim of the same lengthy neglect.

In the several days since my arrival, I've observed that time has stood still in Cuba. This is evident throughout the country, but especially in Havana, which was once one of the most vibrant cities in the Western world. Its gaiety, laugher, and excitement have long been muted, and it is obvious that Hemingway's Eden is gone, maybe forever. The only visible reminder

161

of his existence here is the *Finca Vigia*, his former home. It is now Museo Ernest Hemingway—The Ernest Hemingway Museum.

A few places evoke flashbacks to his time on the island, though. I experienced one when I was shooting white-winged doves and ducks in the Pinar del Rio province, the rice country where Hemingway often hunted. Another day while fishing out of the Bay of Pigs, I remembered a letter to Janet Flanner in 1933 in which he described the Cuban coast:

> It is wonderful. The gulf stream runs almost black and comes right in to the shore. The marlin swordfish go by, swimming up the stream like cars on a highway. You go in to shore in the boat and look down and see the wrinkles in the white sand through the clear water. It looks as though you would strike bottom and when you drop anchor the rope won't reach bottom. They have beaches miles and miles long, hard white sand and no houses for twenty miles.

I doubt that when I leave I will have regrets—unless they are for what used to be.

◆   ◆   ◆

MARLIN FISHING HAD been on Hemingway's mind almost since the time he came to Key West. At Sloppy Joe's Bar, Josie Russell told him stories of the giant billfish in the waters off the Cuban coast. Russell had often seen monster marlin caught by commercial fishermen when he was on rum-running trips between Havana and Key West. The more tales Russell told, the more eager Hemingway became.

He no doubt heard more about this bonanza of huge marlin from Carlos Gutierrez, the fishing boat captain he met in the Dry Tortugas in 1929. Gutierrez had the reputation of having boated more marlin in the previous fifteen years than any other commercial fisherman out of Havana's harbor.

He got his chance in April 1932. Russell knew the best time for marlin was approaching, and he agreed to accompany Hemingway on a fishing trip to Cuba on the *Anita*. Because they went as friends, sharing the responsibilities and fishing action, Russell charged only half the usual charter fee.

The trip was supposed to be for two weeks, but it ended up lasting two months. The fishing was excellent, and as if that weren't enough, the night life in Havana was lively and exciting. Besides, renovation of the house on Whitehead Street was far from complete, and Hemingway rationalized that little writing could be accomplished until the work was over. Instead, he took a room at the Ambos Mundos Hotel and between cruises worked on galley proofs of *Death in the Afternoon*. He also found time to write "Now I Lay Me," another of his Nick Adams stories.

During the Cuban holiday Pauline came over twice, and Charles Thompson and Bra Saunders also joined them. Hemingway enlisted Carlos Gutierrez to serve as his chief consultant.

From the beginning, marlin fishing excited and intrigued Hemingway. It was eventually to become the sport most closely associated with his name: a sort of trademark. It is logical that it would have, because no other fish offers such a variety of challenges or provides a more spectacular trophy. Billfishermen—and they are a special breed—look upon marlin as the Cadillacs of big-game fish, and those with sufficient wealth travel the world fishing for different species.

Probably what most aroused Hemingway's fierce competitive spirit was that marlin have enormous power and stamina and attain weights of well over a thousand pounds. He was proud of his own bull strength and wanted to pit himself against these monsters. But that was at the outset. Once this desire was satisfied, he began to develop strategies and techniques for fighting marlin that were revolutionary. Other anglers adopted them, but what they couldn't match was the muscle.

Hemingway's exhilaration over the sensational Cuban fishing is evident in a letter he wrote to John Dos Passos in May 1932. Dos Passos had been invited along but couldn't make it.

Well you played it wrong not to make this trip. Damn I wish you could have made it. Have caught 19 Martin Swordfish and 3 sailfish (one 8 feet 9 inches). Been feeding the whole waterfront. It sells for 10 cents a pound even in these times. We've given them all away—cut 'em up and hand 'em out when we come in. But to hell with feeding the waterfront. You ought to see them strike Dos. Jump more than tarpon and fast as light— one jumped 23 times. Charles fought one 2 hours 5 minutes then hook pulled loose when he went to gaff him. Fish ran out 500 yards of line 3 times. Have to chase them with the boat hooked up—them jumping all the time throwing water like a racing motor boat in a sea. Have had 17 strikes in a day—never less than 3. Biggest we've caught so far a little over nine feet— caught 2 today—Sat. 4—caught 30 lb dolphin.

When the summer ended, Hemingway went back to Wyoming and afterward to New York, but in 1933 when the April moon began to wax toward full, he chartered the *Anita* for another two-month stay in Cuba. Russell again went along, and once they reached Cuba, Hemingway at once retained Carlos Gutierrez. His one regret was that Dos Passos, Strater, and some of his other fishing pals were not along to share the fun and excitement. Bumby was visiting for the summer, and he made occasional trips over from Key West with Pauline to go out with his father.

The main marlin migration had not yet begun, so the early fishing was slow. By late May, Hemingway wrote Arnold Gingrich that he had caught twenty-nine marlin, including a one-day total of seven, which he thought might be a record. A few days later things had improved greatly, because in a letter to Henry Strater Hemingway tells of seeing a hundred marlin in one day and having eighteen strikes.

The Cuban trip again exceeded the planned length, and by late July, Hemingway had spent nearly a hundred days on the Gulf Stream. Yet as on the first trip, all was not play. Marlin run on the filling moon when the tides are strongest, and they drop off when it begins to wane. When the action slowed, he retreated to his room at the Ambos Mundos Hotel and worked.

Several important projects were in progress. Arnold Gingrich had assigned him to do a series of nonfiction articles on hunting and fishing for his new magazine, *Esquire*. Hemingway was gathering material for the first of these as well as information for a nonfiction book he planned to do on the mysteries of the Gulf Stream. He had also begun work on a long short story, "One Trip Across," that would later appear in *Cosmopolitan*. In the midst of all these chores, he had to choose a title for his new book of short stories. In June, he decided on *Winner Take Nothing*. On July 26, after his return to Key West, Hemingway wrote Perkins to wind up their business affairs before his departure for Spain and on to the African safari. He included a summation of his recent fishing achievements:

> Poor old Hem the fragile one. 99 days in the sun on the gulf stream. 54 swordfish. Seven in one day. A 468 pounder in 65 minutes, alone, no help except them holding me around the waist and pouring buckets of water on my head. Two hours and 20 minutes of straight hell with another. A 343 pounder that jumped 44 times, hooked in the bill. I killed him in an hour and forty five minutes. Poor fragile old Hem posing as a fisherman again.

The delivery of the *Pilar* in the spring of 1934 allowed Hemingway to plan his next Cuban venture along whatever lines he wished. He wanted Josie Russell along, but Russell could not get away. Prohibition had ended and he was too busy handling the booming business at his bar. Carlos Gutierrez had again been signed on, along with a cook named Juan. The other member of the party was Arnold Samuelson, the young admirer from Minnesota who Hemingway had befriended but who had no talents as a crew member.

This trip provided an unusual mixture of activities, although the fishing wasn't particularly good except for the final day when Hemingway caught a twelve-foot, 420-pound marlin that took him an hour and fifteen minutes to boat. There were, however, other things to occupy the time. Hemingway had invited Charles Calwalder, director of the Academy of Natural Sciences of Philadelphia, and Henry W. Fowler, his chief ichthyologist, to join him and study the habits of marlin and identify the different species. They went out on the *Pilar* every day for a month. Fowler said the knowledge he gained was enough to permit him to revise marlin classification for the entire North Atlantic. It was the first of Hemingway's contributions to the scientific community and the International Game Fish Association.

During this period there were numerous visitors aboard the *Pilar,* among them Charles and Lorine Thompson, Grant and Jane Mason, and a Cuban painter, Antonio Gattorno. As usual, Pauline shuttled back and forth.

The African book was not top priority, but Hemingway continued to work on it. By late August it had reached twenty-three thousand words. He returned to Key West in early September, then went back to Cuba and fished until late October with only minimal success.

The discovery of Bimini and the sport of fishing for giant bluefin tuna occupied Hemingway during 1935, but in late April 1936, he set out again for Cuba, accompanied by Josie Russell. The fishing was poor, and the *Pilar* developed engine trouble. In addition, Carlos Gutierrez had failing eyesight and hearing, minimizing his capabilities as a gaffman. Russell went back to Key West in mid-May, and soon after Hemingway took the *Pilar* to Miami for repairs.

It was 1939 before Hemingway was again in Cuba. In the years between he had been involved in two wars: the Spanish Civil War and the domestic conflict that was soon to end his marriage to Pauline. His encounter with Martha Gelhorn in Sloppy Joe's Bar in December 1936 had quickly evolved into a romance, most of which was conducted while they both were correspondents in Spain.

In February 1939 Hemingway returned to Cuba and moved back into the Ambos Mundos Hotel. Writing was on his mind, and he first finished a short story he had begun. Then, on March 1, he began what was to become one of his most important works—a novel about the Spanish Civil War. He visited Key West in late March to see Bumby, then came back to Havana in early April.

Soon afterward Martha joined him with full intention of staying permanently. Hemingway had agreed to look for a house, but upon her arrival, she found that he had not done so. Within a short time, Martha found a somewhat rundown estate a dozen miles southeast of Havana in the village of San Francisco de Paula. It was called *Finca Vigia*—Lookout Farm—and could be rented for one hundred dollars a month.

Although Hemingway at first balked at the property because of its shabby condition, he eventually relented. Once moved from his quarters in the Ambos Mundos, he found it quite suitable and adapted quickly. At this point the Spanish Civil War novel was progressing rapidly, and he was diligently sticking to his writing routine.

All was sunny in Cuba, but settling in at the *Finca* was a major move toward the ultimate break with Pauline.

17

A TURBULENT TIME

WORLD WAR II INTERRUPTED Hemingway's placid and productive existence in Cuba. He survived dangerous duty as a foreign correspondent, but his union with Martha did not. Both were extremely strong-willed, and theirs proved to be a collaboration that was destined to fail.

As in the case of his two earlier marriages, Hemingway had a successor chosen before the split with Martha occurred. This time it was a fellow journalist, Mary Welch, whom he met in London during the blitz. She was also married, but this did not deter their romance. They planned a future together and decided to proceed with it regardless of their individual marital situations.

After the war ended, Hemingway came back to the *Finca* and dedicated himself to restoring the house and grounds. Two months later, Mary joined him and became the new "lady of the house," which Hemingway had equipped with a staff that included a Chinese cook, a chauffeur, maids, a butler, gardeners, and a couple of errand boys. Mary proved to be an efficient manager, and she quickly transformed the *Finca* into the most comfortable and luxurious abode Hemingway had ever known. By the end of 1945, both divorces had been granted, and Hemingway and Mary exchanged vows on March 14, 1946.

Life in Cuba was quite different from Key West. Instead of writers and artists and people of moderate means. Hemingway's friends and fishing companions in Havana were wealthy sportsmen with backgrounds in business and the military. Two of these, Mayito Menocal and Ellicio Arguelles, were often with him on the *Pilar* or at pigeon shoots and social events.

Both men admired Hemingway and spoke highly of him. In later years, Menocal's son declared that Hemingway "was a man who enhanced life, in the Arab sense, for all his friends. Things became more enjoyable when done with him or looked at through his eyes. . . . He managed to imbue the most trivial sporting activity with his own sense of the challenging and dramatic."

Arguelles's recollection was quite similar: "I have never known a man who enjoyed life more. He did everything to the fullest."

Hemingway's life was changed in other ways as well. *For Whom the Bell Tolls* had made Hemingway both wealthy and even more famous, so he was given special status in social and sporting circles. His affluence allowed him to lead a life of leisure. With the *Pilar* moored at Havana Harbor or at Cojimar, he could fish at will, either alone with his crew or with whatever companions he chose. An additional pleasure was that Havana was a virtual Western Paris, with a glittering nightlife frequented by what in subsequent generations would be known as "beautiful people."

Unlike during the years with Pauline on Whitehead Street, fishing was no longer Hemingway's consuming passion. His prominence as a literary figure took a toll on his time, and once settled in after the war years, he began work on *The Garden of Eden*, a strange novel that did not come to completion during his lifetime. Writing occupied most of 1946, both in Cuba and for a time during the winter in Sun Valley.

Personal and family illness and the deaths of friends plagued Hemingway during 1947, and both fishing and writing were held to a virtual standstill. In the fall he escaped once again to Sun Valley. Mary joined him later along with his three boys and some other guests. The sojourn proved so enjoyable that they stayed until January.

The next year, 1948, was better all around. In June, Hemingway arranged a fishing trip to the Bahamas aboard Mayito Menocal's luxury yacht, the *Delicias*. The party included Mary, his sons Patrick and Gregory, Menocal, and Elicio Arguelles. The trip lasted ten days, and by Hemingway's account, during three five-hour stretches of trolling they averaged taking a fish every three minutes. It was a varied catch, including marlin, kingfish, amberjack, wahoo, albacore, yellowtail, grouper, and barracuda.

On his own ventures he did well also. He wrote his publisher, Charles Scribner, that in June he had caught "18 good dolphin, 5 good wahoos, 6 kingfish (one 54 lbs.), a 48-pound snapper, and 7 marlin. The largest a 110 lb. white marlin on 15 thread line and a feather jig."

Another long cruise took place in July, but no serious fishing was undertaken. The purpose was mainly to celebrate Hemingway's forty-ninth birthday, and a party atmosphere prevailed.

As Hemingway plunged further into the life of a celebrity, fishing became less important. In earlier days it had been both his favorite way to relax and his best means of getting away from distractions. Now he spent more time projecting himself into public view. The Hemingway legend was growing, and he enjoyed nurturing it.

The trip to Italy that occupied the latter part of 1948 and the early months of 1949 resulted in the birth of the idea for a new novel, *Across the River and into the Trees*, and Hemingway worked on it steadily once he was back in Cuba. He interrupted it to make two fishing trips, one a relative bust because of circumstances and the other primarily a social venture.

The Hemingways returned to Europe in 1950, dividing their time between Paris, Venice, and Cortina. He completed the novel in Paris and was jubilant with what he saw as another huge success. Upon publication the following September, however, it was given dismal reviews.

Hemingway's disappointment was short-lived though, and his writing energy was renewed after a couple of months. In a remarkable working streak that lasted for more than three weeks, he "completed" *The Sea When Absent*, the second book in his proposed sea trilogy. (It was actually incomplete and eventually became part of the posthumously published *Islands in the Stream*.) He finished the draft on Christmas Eve, and once the holiday season was over, he began work on the story idea that had been on his mind since it was told to him by Carlos Gutierrez in 1935—the old Cuban fisherman who battles a giant marlin.

The writing went amazingly fast. By mid-January he had produced six thousand words, and the novella was virtually done by mid-February. During one stretch Hemingway produced more than a thousand words a day for sixteen straight days, twice his usual output.

The book was, of course, *The Old Man and the Sea*, finished in 1951 and in typescript for a year before its publication. When it finally appeared, the result was the greatest critical acclaim, awards, and public fanfare of his entire career.

Although many readers and reviewers saw the book as heavily symbolic, Hemingway flatly denied it. In a letter to his friend Bernard Berenson in September 1952, he wrote:

There isn't any symbolysm [*sic*]. The sea is the sea. The old man is an old man. The boy is a boy and the fish is a fish. The sharks are all sharks no better and no worse. All the symbolism that people say is shit. What goes beyond is what you see beyond when you know. A writer should know too much.

In the same letter he also described a recent fishing trip and the feelings it elicited:

We have a wonderful current in the Gulf still in spite of the
changes in weather and we have 29 good fish so far. Now they are
all very big and each one is wonderful and different. I think you
would like it very much; the leaving of the water and the entering
into it of the huge fish moves me as much as the first time I ever
saw it. I always told Mary that on the day I did not feel happy
when I saw a flying fish leave the water I would quit fishing.

In the spring of 1953, *The Old Man and the Sea* won the
Pulitzer Prize for fiction just as Hemingway was completing plans
for a second African safari. He also wanted to visit Spain again to
see how the country was faring under the Franco regime. The
Spanish portion of the journey went well, as did most of the
African adventure. Near the end, however, disaster overtook
them. Hemingway and Mary were in two small plane crashes in
succession. The first crash left both of them only slightly hurt, but
it resulted in the erroneous report that Hemingway had been
killed. The second crash was far more serious. It came close to
ending his life. His injuries included his fifth concussion, a fractured skull, ruptured liver, kidney, and spleen, internal bleeding, a
dislocated shoulder and arm, and first-degree burns.

Hemingway had chartered a boat for a fishing expedition off
the Kenya coast before the accidents. Despite his poor physical
condition, he insisted on going through with the plans, even
though he seldom participated in the fishing. In March, Hemingway went to Venice for further medical consultation and treatment. Before departing, he and Mary made a swing through
Spain, then returned to Genoa and sailed for home.

Back at the *Finca*, Hemingway was determined to fight himself back to good health again. His spirits were lifted considerably
in late October 1954 when he received word he had been
awarded the Nobel Prize.

Final plans to begin filming *The Old Man and the Sea* were
responsible for getting him back in shape again. He wanted to

participate in the action in order to provide advice and assure as much authenticity as possible. Shooting began in August 1955, but two months of fishing Cuban waters failed to produce the action shots necessary. Hemingway caught several marlin, but even though some jumped suitably, they were too small.

In April 1956, operations were moved to Peru in the hope that the Humboldt Current would produce the huge marlin they required. Again, bad luck prevailed, and no suitable action shots were obtained. In the end, much of the footage was shot with a fake marlin and fake sharks built in Hollywood. The real marlin footage, purchased from Alfred Glassell, was a chronicle of his catch of the 1,560-pound, world-record black marlin.

It was Hemingway's last serious quest for big fish, and the futility of it left him disappointed and unhappy. During 1957 and 1958 the political situation in Cuba was becoming increasingly unsettled. At first, Hemingway felt no threat, but eventually he realized that the changes were heralding his withdrawal from the place in the sun he loved so much. His last visit was in the summer of 1959. As Leicester Hemingway explains in his book, *My Brother, Ernest Hemingway*, it ended on a sour note:

> When he returned, he reactivated the annual spring marlin tournaments he had organized in 1951 and continued for several years until political conditions grew intolerable. The spring of Fidel's triumph, Ernest officially presented the bearded dictator with a trophy and was quoted as saying, "You may be new at fishing, but you're a lucky fisherman." It was common knowledge during the tournament that Dr. Castro had one of the insular champions aboard his boat and the champion had been observed hooking a fish and then passing the rod to someone else. After the tournament, Ernest had a bad taste in his mouth. He knew he had been used.

PART 5

The West

18
WYOMING

IN A LOG CABIN on a ranch in the northwestern corner of Wyoming is an old school desk. It is the kind I remember from my youth: slightly slanted with a hole for an inkwell, a groove for a pencil, and a hinged top under which is space for books and other supplies.

Under ordinary circumstances seeing this piece of furniture would elicit only a minor ripple of nostalgia. In this case, though, it's different. I'm on what was once the L-Bar-T—the Nordquist ranch—and this is the cabin in which Hemingway stayed in 1932 on his second trip to the West.

At that time he was hard at work on *Death in the Afternoon*, and that's where the desk comes in. It's easy to visualize him sitting there writing longhand, stopping occasionally to rest his eyes and look out at the majestic peaks of Pilot and Index Mountains silhouetted against the blue Wyoming sky.

Of course, there's no way of knowing if the desk was there originally. Perhaps it was. On the other hand, maybe Lawrence Nordquist thought it would be useful to Hemingway and added it for that purpose. It's even possible that Hemingway himself was responsible for its presence. In any case, for me it served a purpose by just being there.

◆　◆　◆

AT KEY WEST IN mid-June 1928, Hemingway was halfway through the first draft of A *Farewell to Arms* and talking to his friend Charles Thompson about wanting to go west to a place where he could complete the book and do some trout fishing. He was also hoping to escape the humidity and upcoming hurricane season.

The impending birth of Pauline's first baby provided the ideal opportunity. Since the medical facilities in Key West were limited, Pauline wanted her doctor in Kansas City to deliver the child. This location was also closer to her family home in Arkansas, where she planned to go to recuperate.

So they drove from Key West to Kansas City, where Patrick was born on June 28. Hemingway continued to work on his novel during Pauline's hospital stay, bringing the manuscript to 478 pages. When she was released, he took her and the baby by train to Piggot and then returned to Kansas City. He had arranged to meet Bill Horne, an old pal, who would accompany him to Wyoming. His original plan had been to go to the Salmon River in Idaho, but since Wyoming was somewhat closer, he decided to put the Idaho trip on hold until later.

The pair made the long trip in three days and checked in at Eleanor Donnelly's Upper Folly ranch near Sheridan on July 30. Good trout fishing was readily available, but to Hemingway's dismay fifteen girls had signed in as guests. He became disgusted and departed on August 3. He checked into the Sheridan Inn, and four days later he moved again, this time to the Lower Folly ranch, at which no dudes were staying. His routine there was to write in the morning and fish in the afternoon. He found that both endeavors were paying off.

Once Pauline was fit again, she left Patrick with her family and headed west to join her husband. She arrived in Sheridan on

Pilot and Index Peaks provide a magnificent backdrop to the cabin used by the Hemingways. The Yellowstone River's Clarks Fork, a great trout stream, is only a few hundred yards away.

August 18, and they went to Willis Spear's Spear-O-Wigwam dude ranch in a primitive setting near what is now the Cloud Peak Primitive Area in the Bighorn National Forest. Hemingway was on the final stretch of the novel, and after several days of intense effort at the Wigwam ranch, he advised Max Perkins at Scribner's that the first draft was complete.

Willis Spear's daughter, Elsa Spear Byron, was approaching her ninety-fifth birthday when she gave me her recollections of the Hemingways' visit.

"They came to the ranch when I was on a pack trip with eight women, so they were there when I came back. He'd come out earlier and stayed at both of Eleanor Donnelly's ranches and at a hotel in Sheridan. After Pauline arrived, they came up to the Wigwam.

"At first I didn't see much of him except at mealtime, but I found him to be a very pleasant person. He liked to visit with everybody. However, his main purpose was to finish A *Farewell to Arms*, so he spent most of his time in his cabin. He didn't even seem to have much interest in fishing.

"When the book was done, we saw more of him. Once he could relax, he and Pauline went fishing every day. There are plenty of streams and lakes near the camp, and they usually had good luck. When the ranch closed for the season, Hemingway and Pauline decided to go farther west and visit some other places. I think they first stayed at a cabin on Wolf Mountain. I never saw Hemingway after that, but I used to get letters from Pauline. I liked her. She was a nice person and devoted to her husband.

"That was more than sixty years ago, but some things haven't changed. The Wigwam is still there and open from the first of June through Labor Day. I haven't been up there in a long time. Also, the road to the Wigwam was always pretty scary, and I understand it still is, so that hasn't changed, either."

Hemingway talked about this particular period in a letter he wrote to Waldo Pierce on August 23, 1928:

> Pauline came out and I finished the damn book, first draft—finally. Then we fished, caught 30 apiece every day, none over 15 inches, but damn nice trout. This is a cockeyed wonderful country, looks like Spain, swell people. Every time I go out and see it I wish you were here to paint it.

Hemingway and Pauline made a swing through the Tetons and fished the Snake River, then stopped off at Shell on their way back to Sheridan to visit with Owen Wister, author of *The Virginian*. They were back in Kansas City on September 23. As usual, Hemingway kept a fishing log, and at the end of the trip he noted that the number of trout he and Pauline had caught during their month of western angling was six hundred—exactly the number of pages in his recently completed manuscript.

◆　　◆　　◆

THERE WAS NO OPPORTUNITY to go west in 1929. Hemingway and Pauline went to Europe in April and remained for the rest of the year, shuttling between Paris, Pamplona, and Switzerland. He returned to Key West in February, but anticipating the eventual rise in humidity, he laid plans for another trip to Wyoming where he could work on his bullfighting book and fish. Bumby was coming to spend the summer, and when he arrived, Hemingway picked him up at the pier, then drove straight to Piggot to collect Pauline. Hemingway wanted to go farther west this time, so he made inquiries in Sheridan and was referred to Simon Snyder's ranch near Painter.

Things might have worked out there if he could have remained anonymous; however, someone found out who he was, and he became a focus of attention. Irritated by such distractions, he packed up and headed to another ranch a few miles farther west. The family rolled into Lawrence and Olive Nordquist's L-Bar-T ranch on July 13.

He couldn't have found a place that would better afford him the mix of privacy and limited fellowship that he craved. Yet that was only one of its many advantages. Nordquist's spread was in an isolated corner of Wyoming just a few miles from the old mining town of Cooke City, Montana, and close to the boundary of Yellowstone. The country is scenically spectacular, with the ranch in a long valley flanked by peaks that rise to elevations of more than ten thousand feet and through which the fast, clear Clarks Fork of the Yellowstone flows.

The river instantly commanded Hemingway's attention. It was teeming with rainbows and just a short stroll from the new double cabin Nordquist moved them into. He not only had an ideal place to work but also a perfect spot to go when he wanted to relax. Hemingway had discovered another paradise.

For the first couple of weeks he was somewhat torn between working on the bullfighting book and fishing the Clarks Fork. At the beginning of August, however, heavy rains began to fall, and before midmonth he had written more than forty thousand words. When the torrents ceased, the work-play routine resumed.

Bumby was then almost seven years old and already preferring to be called Jack. He says in his book, *Misadventures of a Fly Fisherman*, that his father and Pauline usually went fishing in the mornings after breakfast. They would pack a lunch and saddle up horses, heading for likely spots downstream. Sometimes when his father fished close to the lodge, Jack was allowed to watch if he stayed inconspicuous and didn't spook the trout.

Jack was obsessed with the idea of catching a trout, but he did not accomplish that feat until a few days before they departed, when he was allowed to fish with Pauline's outfit:

> Nevertheless, I learned a lot about casting and about playing fish once they were hooked. Papa was a pretty straightforward wet-fly fisherman. He used Hardy tackle and his leaders were already made up with three flies. His favorites were a McGinty for the top, a *cock-y-bondhu* for the middle, and a woodcock green and yellow for the tail fly. He sometimes fished with single-eyed flies and added a dropper. At the ranch, for these, he preferred a Hardy's worm fly and the shrimp fly.
>
> Ninety percent of the time, Papa was an across and downstream caster whose team of flies swam or skittered across the current so that a taking fish pretty much hooked himself. He played the fish gently and well and with the necessary calm that eliminates hurrying a fish too fast or laying it too long, which is just as great a sin.

Bill Horne and his wife, Bunny, whom Bill had met when he was with Hemingway at the Donnelly ranch in 1929, came to spend two weeks at the L-Bar-T. The day after they arrived there was a break in the weather, and Hemingway and Bill took forty-nine good trout. The rains resumed, and the stream did not clear up until just before the Hornes left on August 22, when Hemingway, Pauline,

*The Nordquist Ranch provided Hemingway both a private hideaway for
writing and a river filled with trout.*

Bill, and Bunny caught a total of thirty. It was the Hornes' grand finale, but not Hemingway's. In one three-day period during the last days of August he took a total of ninety-two trout.

He killed two bears in late August, then after Pauline and Bumby left for New York on September 14, he went hunting again for elk and mountain sheep. Yet even with the interruptions, he still managed to complete two hundred pages of the bullfighting book by September 28.

It had been a good summer and fall, but it ended on a discordant note. He was headed home on November 10 when he was involved in a car accident that left him with a badly fractured right arm. The break required surgery and a lengthy hospital stay in Billings, Montana. He did not get back to Key West until just before Christmas.

The next year, 1931, Pauline's second child was due in November, but Hemingway needed to gather more material for the bullfighting book. So he devised an itinerary that took them to France in May, on to Spain for the bullfights from June through September, then back to New York until it was time to go to Kansas City for the delivery of the baby. Once again, they were back in Key West in December. They moved into the new home on Whitehead Street that Pauline's Uncle Gus had purchased for them.

The European trip paid off well. In mid-January, Hemingway advised Perkins that he had finished *Death in the Afternoon*.

◆　◆　◆

WHEN HEMINGWAY AND PAULINE came back to the Nordquist ranch in July 1932, he did not have a novel to serve as a preoccupation, only the reading of page proofs of *Death in the Afternoon*. This freedom from pressure permitted plenty of time to explore new fishing sites, particularly tributaries of the Clarks Fork and some of the high lakes that required long rides on horseback to reach.

He was troubled, however, by construction the state had begun on a road from Red Lodge, Montana, to Cooke City across Beartooth Pass. He saw this project as an intrusion into this land of plenty that would eventually destroy the fishing and hunting. A road builder's dam had already dried up one fork of a favorite stream.

The possibility that he might never enjoy this utopia again caused him to fish with increased fervor. His log shows 333 trout were taken between July 15 and September 6 by Hemingway and those who fished with him.

Gerald and Sara Murphy and their two children came to visit in early September, and he took them on a fishing trip to the Crazy Lakes in the high country. At that time, Charles Thompson also joined Hemingway to do some hunting, and when the Murphys and Pauline had gone, they headed out on a pack trip. On October 16, after bagging an elk and a black bear apiece, they set out for home in a blizzard.

Three years passed before Hemingway and Pauline got back to Wyoming. Much had taken place in the interval, including an African safari, the delivery of the *Pilar,* and the writing of *Green Hills of Africa* and a collection of short stories, *Winner Take Nothing.*

Hemingway, Pauline, Bumby, and Patrick crossed the plank bridge over the Clarks Fork at the L-Bar-T ranch on August 10, 1936. This time Lawrence Nordquist put them in the Sidley Cabin, quarters that offered more room and comfort. Hemingway had used it before as a backup refuge in which to escape and write.

This time there was another novel in progress, *To Have and Have Not.* Hemingway worked on it intermittently during the rest of August and most of September. He had persuaded a couple he knew from Bimini, Tommy and Lorainne Shevlin, to come and experience the wonderful environment. They joined the Hemingways on a fishing trip to Granite Lake and later on hunted for antelope and grizzly bears. The Shevlins left for California in late September, and Hemingway returned to his novel, hoping to complete it before it was time to return to Key West.

He did not make it, although he determined he'd written around fifty thousand words since his arrival at the ranch in August. After months of indecision and arguing with Perkins, the novel was finally set in type in June 1937.

◆　◆　◆

PAULINE WAS ABROAD IN August 1939 when Hemingway decided to go back to Wyoming with Bumby. He was well into a new novel, with seventy-six thousand words written, and, not unknown to Pauline, well into a relationship with Martha Gelhorn.

This time there was not much fishing opportunity. He had scarcely arrived when Pauline called from New York and said she was flying out to join him. The reunion was not a happy one. Hemingway made the final break, packed the car, and arranged to have Pauline and the boys driven home. He had Martha meet him in Billings, and they drove on to a new resort in Idaho—Sun Valley.

◆　◆　◆

WHEN I VISITED THE area I found that the ranch is no longer known as the L-Bar-T. It is in private ownership and has not been operated commercially for many years. Lawrence Nordquist is long dead and only a distant memory in the minds of a few of the oldest local residents. Olive Nordquist, however, owned and operated a small motel in Cooke City until her death in the late 1980s. She's well remembered, particularly by Ralph Glidden, a local historian who owns the Cooke City Store. As a teenager, he used to help her around the motel. He says she was very fond of the Hemingways and often talked about them.

The highway over Beartooth Pass may have had an impact on the fishing and hunting, but it did not ruin it. The Clarks Fork is still an excellent trout stream, and there's good hunting in the area, even though the limits are not as generous and the seasons not as long. And the old mining town of Cooke City may be a little larger today, though that's debatable. By any measure, it is still small.

19

SUN VALLEY

HE IS STANDING OUTSIDE a weathered store building alongside
Silver Creek, a stern-faced old man with a .22 rifle in his hand.
As I pull up beside him, I ask if he shoots strangers.

"Nope. I'm after starlings. They're real pests, you know."

A bird flies by overhead, and he follows it with his eyes then
looks back at me.

"Wrong kind. That's a yellow-headed blackbird. They hang
around near water."

It is 10:00 A.M., but there is no sign of activity in the store.
When I ask about it, he tells me, "It was my store, and it's closed.
My wife's not well, and we're going to have to move to a place
that suits her health better."

I tell him my reason for stopping is that I was told in Sun
Valley that this store was a place where fishermen congregated.
Hemingway was supposed to have been one of them.

"Yeah, he came by sometimes. I remember him well. There
wasn't anything unusual about him. He was just like the other bums

Hemingway found that beautiful Silver Creek was not far from Sun Valley, but he never fished here. He did hunt in the area, however.

who came in after they were through fishing to drink beer and tell lies."

He is smiling, so I know the comment is mostly in jest.

"Come inside," he says. "I've got some newspaper clippings I can show you."

He produces them, and I look forward to seeing ones that refer to Hemingway. It doesn't happen. They are about various other things, and it makes me wonder. As a matter of conversation, I comment that he must have been operating the store for a long time.

"Sure have. Twenty-seven years. I first came here in 1963."

I do a mental double-take and ask him to repeat the date.

"Yep. 1963. I'll show you a clipping that tells about it."

I'm a bit deflated, but I look, anyway. The newspaper story verifies the information. I thank him for his time and depart. I see no reason to mention to him that Hemingway died in 1961.

◆   ◆   ◆

SUN VALLEY WAS HARDLY the place for Hemingway to keep his relationship with Martha low profile, because, once there, he was in the publicity spotlight. And anyway, considering that the affair had been conducted openly in Spain, he had no great desire to hide it.

The resort, along with the little town that bore its name, was built by Averell Harriman, owner of the Union Pacific Railroad, as a plush destination for skiers. He had traveled in Europe and had noted the popularity of the ski resorts in the Swiss and Austrian Alps. Harriman hoped to develop one in the American West to increase wintertime use of the railroad.

He enlisted a young Austrian count, Felix Schaffgotch, to conduct a study to find the best site. After searching through California's Sierra Range, the area around Salt Lake City, and the Colorado Rockies, Schaffgotch discovered an ideal spot in the vicinity of the small mining town of Ketchum, Idaho.

From the time of its opening in 1936, the resort has promoted itself by hosting a long succession of Hollywood stars and other celebrities. The management was aware of Hemingway's reputation as a writer and sportsman, so they offered to pay all of his expenses at the resort for the privilege of using his name for publicity. Upon the break with Pauline in September 1939, and given the need for a place where he and Martha could be together, he found the Sun Valley proposition easy to accept.

Once Hemingway and Martha were established in suite 206 in the Sun Valley Lodge, he resumed work on the new novel. Since he had the pleasant obligation to pose for publicity pictures, he continued his familiar routine of writing in the morning and playing in the afternoons.

There was plenty of opportunity for the latter. The country around Sun Valley and Ketchum abounded with excellent trout streams and a variety of game birds—pheasants, ducks, doves, snipe, sage grouse, and chukars. Lloyd Arnold, the company photographer and an avid outdoorsman, was responsible for setting up the activities, which usually involved Taylor "Beartracks" Williams, Sun Valley's chief guide.

The first year, Hemingway's companions other than Arnold and Williams were Martha, other guests at the lodge, and some local ranchers. This scenario would change radically. In the fall of 1941 he hunted with Gary Cooper, with whom he formed a close and lasting friendship. Later, as his involvement with the movie industry grew, he became friends with some of its most prominent personalities, among them Howard Hawks, Leland Hayward, Margaret Sullavan, Ingrid Bergman, Clark Gable, Robert Taylor, and Barbara Stanwyck. Most important, starting in 1941, his sons were able to join him and he could pass along the legacy of outdoor togetherness he had inherited from his father.

There is something of a myth surrounding Hemingway's angling adventures in Idaho; in fact, he did far less fishing there than is supposed. Hunting became his main interest, and most of his outdoor adventures were with a gun, not a rod. What created part of the misconception were publicity shots taken by Arnold in the fall of 1939. They show him fighting a fish and posing with a pair of nice rainbows that were supposedly taken on Silver Creek, a stream not far from Sun Valley.

Information in Arnold's book, *Hemingway: High on the Wild*, indicates that they were actually taken elsewhere. Gene Van Guilder, who was in charge of publicity for Sun Valley Lodge, wanted to do a press release on Hemingway. As Arnold writes:

> A fishing trip was organized soon after with Pop Marks to act as guide. He selected Big Wood River below Magic Reservoir, splendid water for nice rainbow trout. There was a bug in that deal, though. In a grove of cottonwoods a short way upstream from the action, a very dead critter made the air thick enough to cut with a knife. The stench was almost unbearable, but the place was right. I got one action shot of Ernest fighting the fish, and on the posed shots, Gene stood by with a red bandana handkerchief tied over his face, just his eyes twinkling above it.

*When I visited the suite used by Hemingway at the Sun Valley Lodge in
1940 where he did the final work on* For Whom the Bell Tolls, *I could not
resist the urge to sit at his table and record my thoughts.*

Ernest burst out a big guffaw, said, "For Christ's sake, Jesse
James, fetch the bottle of Scotch."

The date was September 28, the one and only time that
Ernest seriously fished for trout in Idaho. He told me later that
the "come hell or high cow" episode had about closed the book
on his freshwater fishing, and that the action picture was the
only one of its kind in existence.

The reason for the slight qualification in using the word "seriously" is that Arnold also mentions earlier in the book that while

191

Trout fishermen find streams like Silver Creek agonizingly unforgiving.

on a picnic at Silver Creek, Hemingway went "dandle [*sic*] fishing" from the bank and caught a nice rainbow.

Jack Hemingway, a consummate fly fisherman, elaborated on this issue one day over lunch at Desperados, a Mexican restaurant in Ketchum, when I brought up the Silver Creek question.

"Arnold is right," he said. "Dad never fished Silver Creek. I'm sure the publicity pictures Lloyd Arnold took are mostly responsible for that notion. After all, Silver Creek isn't far from Sun Valley, and it was the logical place to promote."

192

Yet Hemingway was by no means a stranger to the area, because he often hunted at Silver Creek. It offered great stream jump shooting for ducks, and there were also plenty of snipe in the adjacent marshy bottoms. Today, that part of the creek is a Nature Conservancy Preserve restricted to catch-and-release fly fishing and limited hunting.

The facts notwithstanding, I found it hard to imagine Hemingway not being fascinated by the stream or feeling compelled to fish it. Silver Creek is a classic example of the kind of water that provides a fly fisherman the ultimate challenge in stalking and delicate presentation. It's a slow, meandering meadow stream with long, glassy pools and shallow riffles and reminds me of the chalk streams of southern England: intriguing and exciting, but at the same time, agonizingly unforgiving.

That nagging thought was cleared up when Jack told me of a little-known incident that he sees as the key to his father's change of attitude: "He had a trunk containing all of his prized Hardy trout tackle shipped from Key West to Ketchum by Railway Express, but it never arrived," Jack said. "And the loss affected him to such an extent that he lost all interest in trout fishing after that."

Despite all the outdoor and social activities at Sun Valley and Ketchum, Hemingway had twenty-two chapters of the book finished when he left to go back to Key West in mid-December. When he came back to Sun Valley in September 1940, the novel was complete. He checked into suite 206 once again and began proofreading and making final corrections. While in Key West, working on the last leg of the writing, he had found the title he wanted in a poem by John Donne: *For Whom the Bell Tolls*.

Now that the novel was out of the way, Hemingway devoted his time to hunting when the weather was good and reading when it was bad. Too much company led him to take Martha on a week's pack trip to the Middle Fork of the Salmon River, a place he had once wanted to fish.

With Hemingway's divorce from Pauline finally having come through, he and Martha were married in Cheyenne, Wyoming, on November 21, one day after they left Sun Valley. A busy ten months ensued. They honeymooned in New York then returned to Havana where Hemingway made the purchase of the *Finca* a Christmas present to himself. He claimed to have been driven to Cuba because of the curious hordes of people who had descended upon Key West. The actual motive was to save money on his income tax by establishing nonresident status, which required a six-month absence from the U.S. Martha had been assigned by *Colliers* to cover the war in China, and she persuaded Hemingway to accompany her when she departed in May. They were gone three months, a trip that accomplished half of the nonresident requirement. They came back to the *Finca,* stayed for the remaining three months, then headed back to Sun Valley in late September.

Hemingway spent the remainder of the fall on hunting trips with Martha, his three sons, and his other "family," the Arnolds and the Taylors. It was a glorious period for him. *For Whom the Bell Tolls* had sold half a million copies, the big-game and bird hunting was excellent, and he was surrounded by some of his favorite people.

Hemingway and Martha left Sun Valley in early December on the first leg of their return trip to Cuba. They swung southward and had just crossed the border into Texas when news came over the car radio that would forever change both of their fives: It was December 7, and they learned that the Japanese had bombed Pearl Harbor.

Five years passed before Hemingway again saw Sun Valley. By that time, the war in Europe was over, and so was his marriage to Martha. He returned to his western retreat in 1946 accompanied by his new wife, Mary.

During the war, the Sun Valley Lodge had been used as a rest and rehabilitation center by the navy. Since it was not yet ready for the resumption of commercial operation, the Hemingways

The Big Wood River passes in front of the Hemingway home in Ketchum.

stayed at the McDonald Cabins in Ketchum and hunted and socialized until early November. The 1947 fall visit followed much the same pattern, except that he was at work on *The Garden of Eden*. The progress was slowed by a succession of visitors and, once the snow fell, a renewed interest in skiing. They stayed two weeks longer than planned, finally pulling out of Ketchum on February 1, 1948.

Hemingway's absence from the area lasted more than ten years. During that eventful decade he received both the Pulitzer and Nobel Prizes for literature, and *Across the River and into the Trees* was published. His health, however, had begun to fail, partly due to the many years of excess and his nearly fatal plane crash in Africa.

At first he and Mary rented a house in Ketchum, but in 1959 they purchased the Bob Topping House, a two-story chalet overlooking the Big Wood River. It was his last residence, where he lived until his death.

There is irony here. At one time, having a swift-flowing trout stream virtually in the front yard would have been Hemingway's idea of heaven. But by the time he had realized the dream, fishing was no longer a priority.

He spent a hectic and frustrating summer of 1959 in Spain following the bullfights. Shortly after his return to Ketchum, his long, downhill slide into oblivion began.

EPILOGUE

OCCASIONALLY THERE APPEAR AMONG us larger-than-life individuals who leave an impression on the world that time cannot erase, whose presence seems to linger long after they are gone.

Hemingway was such a person. More than thirty years after his death, his profile is higher than ever before. In death, as in life, the elusive and mysterious Hemingway legend continues to intrigue the public.

Consider the enduring popularity of his work, as well as what has been written about him. Four of his books have been published posthumously—*Islands in the Stream*, *A Moveable Feast*, *The Dangerous Summer*, and *The Garden of Eden*—and there have been countless biographies, recollections by relatives and acquaintances, collections of newspaper dispatches, stories, and articles.

At the heart of this abiding fascination is the Hemingway persona, the product of a dynamic, highly complex, and sometimes outrageous figure. The public saw Hemingway's fictional heroes as Hemingway himself, and his swashbuckling lifestyle fortified that impression. The press eagerly reported his comments and adventures. Today they would say he had star quality.

In truth, Hemingway created his own legend, making it impossible to completely separate the man from the myth.

◆　　◆　　◆

The Hemingway monument, overlooking Trail Creek above the Sun Valley Lodge, is inscribed with excerpts from a eulogy he delivered at a friend's funeral in Ketchum in 1939.

BECAUSE OF HIS EXTRAORDINARY ability to portray so vividly the places he visited, I had a strong sense of déjà vu at each of them. As further credit to his talent for accurate description, in the few places that have remained as they were, I found them to be exactly as I had imagined.

What I experienced in all of the special places in Hemingway's life proved how masterfully accomplished his art was. At every site, I recognized a kind of presence, a feeling much like that of being in charged air after a lightning strike. This sense was particularly strong in Key West, at the old Nordquist ranch, and in suite 206 at Sun Valley Lodge, but it was present to some degree in all of the places.

My imagination? Possibly, but if so, my imagination had been fueled by Hemingway's prose.

◆　　◆　　◆

HEMINGWAY IS BURIED IN the Ketchum Cemetery beneath a marble slab with a simple inscription: Ernest Miller Hemingway, July 21, 1899–July 2, 1961.

A mile and a half up Sun Valley Road from the lodge there is a monument with a bronze bust of Hemingway that was erected in 1966. It stands in a small grove of trees overlooking Trail Creek. Inscribed on the plaque at the base of the monument are words from the eulogy Hemingway wrote following the tragic death of Gene Van Guilder in 1939:

> BEST OF ALL HE LOVED THE FALL
> THE LEAVES YELLOW ON THE COTTONWOODS
> LEAVES FLOATING ON THE TROUT STREAMS
> AND ABOVE THE HILLS
> 　　THE HIGH BLUE WINDLESS SKIES
> . . . NOW HE WILL BE A PART OF THEM FOREVER

It is a fitting tribute, but in reflecting on his life I think also of two lines from "Requiem," a poem by Robert Louis Stevenson. They would serve as an appropriate postscript:

> Home is the sailor, home from the sea,
> And the hunter home from the hill.

SOURCES

Arnold, Lloyd R. *Hemingway: High on the Wild*. New York: Grossett & Dunlap, 1977.

Baker, Carlos. *Ernest Hemingway: A Life Story*. New York: Scribner, 1969.

————, ed. *Ernest Hemingway: Selected Letters, 1917–1961*. New York: Scribner, 1981.

Bellavance-Johnson, Marsha, and Lee Bellavance. *Ernest Hemingway in Idaho: A Guide*. Ketchum, Idaho: The Computer Lab, 1986.

Brian, Denis. *The True Gen: An Intimate Portrait of Ernest Hemingway by Those Who Knew Him*. New York: Grove Press, 1988.

Dorward, Doreen Marsh. *The Sun Valley Story*. Ketchum, Idaho: D. M. Dorward Photography, 1980.

Ferrell, Keith. *Ernest Hemingway: The Search for Courage*. New York: M. Evans, 1984.

Griffin, Peter. *Along With Youth: Hemingway, The Early Years*. New York: Oxford University Press, 1985.

————. *Less Than a Treason: Hemingway in Paris*. New York: Oxford University Press, 1990.

Hemingway, Ernest. *Dateline, Toronto: The Complete Toronto Star Dispatches, 1920–1924*. Edited by William White. New York: Scribner's, 1985.

————. *Death in the Afternoon*. New York: Scribner, 1932.

————. *For Whom the Bell Tolls*. New York: Scribner, 1940.

————. *In Our Time*. New York: Scribner, 1925.

————. *A Moveable Feast*. New York: Scribner, 1964.

Hemingway, Jack. *Misadventures of a Fly Fisherman: My Life With and Without Papa*. Dallas: Taylor Publishing Co., 1986.

Hemingway, Leicester. *My Brother, Ernest Hemingway*. Antioch, Tenn.: World Publishing, 1961.

Johnson, Donald S. "Hemingway: A Trout Fisher's Apprenticeship." *The American Fly Fisherman* (Summer 1989).

———. "Hike to Walloon Lake, June 10–21, 1916, A Diary." *The American Fly Fisherman* (Summer 1989).

Kert, Bernice. *The Hemingway Women*. New York: W. W. Norton, 1983.

Lynn, Kenneth S. *Hemingway*. New York: Simon and Schuster. 1987.

McLendon, James. *Papa: Hemingway in Key West*. Miami: E. A. Seeman Publishing, 1972; reprint, Key West: Langley Press, 1990.

Meyers, Jeffrey. *Hemingway: A Biography*. New York: Harper & Row, 1985.

Reynolds, Michael. *The Young Hemingway*. Cambridge: Basil Blackwell, 1986.

Smedley, Harold Hinsdill. *Trout of Michigan*. N.p.p.: Sportsman's Outdoor Enterprises, 1982.

White, William. *By-Line: Ernest Hemingway, Selected Articles and Dispatches of Four Decades*. New York: Scribner, 1967.

INDEX